The E Factor

**Increase your Career, Business or
Social Enterprise Prospects**

David A Gibson

Published 2006
By Enterprise HQ

Enterprise HQ
Dalton House
60 Windsor Avenue
London
SW19 2RR
www.enterprisehq.co.uk

For any enquiries please contact info@enterprisehq.co.uk

Gibson, David A.
The E Factor – Increase your Career, Business or Social Enterprise Prospects

ISBN 978-0-9553848-0-6
ISBN 0-9553848-0-X

The E Factor

Increase your Career, Business or Social Enterprise Prospects

Contents

Preface

Gordon Brown, the UK Chancellor of the Exchequer stated (HM Treasury 2002) "the education system's potential contribution to making Britain a more entrepreneurial society could be significant, but it is currently neglected". Since that time progress to promote the entrepreneurial society has still remained relatively slow. In particular, there is a need to further develop the enterprise behaviour and employability of students at all levels, not only to encourage small business start up but also to develop a culture of enterprise and innovation.

The National Commission on Entrepreneurship (2004) suggested entrepreneurs have a range of personal characteristics which include risk-taking, vision and confidence. Gibb (2002) also suggested that enterprise skills are very useful not only in starting a business but also to enhance employment prospects. There has thus been a shift both in the further and higher education enterprise curriculum to encourage students to develop 'Enterprise for Life' skills which would be relevant and useful in self-employment, within a company or working within social enterprise. The teaching of enterprise in further and higher education is now inextricably linked to both the enterprise and employability agenda of the government.

In many cases the development of a business plan remains the basis for teaching and assessment within the enterprise curriculum. Although the development of the plan does provide some useful practice in the research and presentation of business information there is a need for a greater focus on the underlying transferable skills which students will be able to use in their business life/career.

The 'E Factor' and its companion workbook provide a model which identifies a generic set of skills designed to enable students achieve success in business or career. These skills are analysed and their relevance to business and social enterprise linked in a practical format.

Students, with the help of the E Factor self assessment questionnaire will be able to identify areas of improvement in entrepreneurship, as well as understand how to apply these skills in practice to develop a range of competencies. Practice in and reflection on the E factor skills provides the potential for students to become more entrepreneurial in whatever career they choose to follow.

At policy level it may also provide the base lever for a change in the enterprise culture and ultimately a more successful and entrepreneurial UK Economy through the creation of more global knowledge businesses supported by entrepreneurial and innovative schools, colleges and universities.

This is a down-to-earth, readable, enjoyable and effective book which will appeal to students of all levels.

Prof. Ken O'Neill BSc (Econ) Hon DSc ACMA FIBA MIoD
Holder of the Queen's Award for Enterprise Promotion – Lifetime Achievement Award

Professor Ken O'Neill is a world-renowned expert in entrepreneurial leadership development and small businesses, he is currently Professor of Entrepreneurship and Small Business Development at the University of Ulster, where he has played a central role over many years in the expansion of the university's pioneering activities in these fields, with particular emphasis on management training and development for owner-managers.

He is the author and editor of numerous books, papers and articles in his field – the most recent being the second edition of the co-authored "Understanding Enterprise, Entrepreneurship and Small Business" (Palgrave Macmillan). He is currently Chairman of Young Enterprise in N.Ireland, the School for Social Entrepreneurs in Ireland and is on the Senate of the Genesis Initiative (a pan-European all-party parliamentary initiative in support of small business).

He is the first person to have been awarded the Queen's Lifetime Achievement Award (2005).

CHAPTER ONE

INNOVATION AND CREATIVITY

INNOVATION AND CREATIVITY

The key skill an Entrepreneur has is his/her ability to spot opportunities, to find markets, and to find innovators to solve problems.

In this era of rapid technological change, the ability to find innovative solutions is a key requirement whether you are in business or not. It is not enough to come up with a new idea for a product or project.

To make your project happen, you will need to be able to overcome unforeseen problems. You need to continuously adapt and innovate in order to move the project forward whatever the difficulties you incur.

Organisations in the past may have been able to follow the same methods of operations for a number of years. Now they have to "go with the flow" and adapt to cope with the pace of change.

So, are you good at coming up with new ideas or do you find it difficult? It is important that you learn how to improve your ability to be creative. This is simply a skill which, like any other requires practice.

Let's do a little test. Have you ever written a poem, a song or appeared in a play? Have you ever drawn a picture?

I defy any of you to say you have never attempted any of these activities! As a child you are encouraged to use your imagination, to play games and have fun. However, once you reach the ages of 11/12, the education system tends to focus on developing your logical and analytical thinking. Unless you excel at art or music, there is little room in the curriculum for helping individuals to come up with new ways to tackle things.

When I teach creativity, I like to set the class a problem which usually involves asking them to come up with new products or services to solve problems. For instance, the task might read: "In groups outline five problems young people between the ages of 18 and 30 have and devise two new products/services to solve these".

Some of the students really struggle initially. They are not attuned to using creativity. Gradually however they start to have fun, suggesting silly ideas and finding innovative solutions all over the place! The group dynamic helps, but gradually the students start to believe that they can make a difference. When you realise that you could come up with an idea which could make a difference, you begin to look at ways of being enterprising and making your idea happen.

The change of attitude this engenders can be really amazing. The problem with training/teaching is that people forget to take the simple steps which can make the difference between developing their thoughts and turning this knowledge into action. I usually get the students to sign an agreement to do three things and I want you to do the same now.

If you keep to this agreement for 30 days, you will increase your chances of being more innovative.

Method needed to articulate
skills.
Why their important
How students can
develop them.

innovation and creativity

Innovation Agreement

I _____ do hereby agree that:

1. I will be more curious and look for unusual connections.

2. I promise to do a few things differently from normal each week

3. I promise to buy a small notebook, take it everywhere for 30 days and write at least one new idea every day

4. Every time I face a problem for the next thirty days, I will ask myself the following questions:

    What can I learn from this?
    What can I do to turn this around?

5   I promise to challenge normal solutions and not make assumptions about people or situations.

Signed _____

Date _____

Please contact me by e-mail and let me know whether you have kept your part of your agreement. If you haven't, please do not read anymore. This book is for doers!

Innovation and Ideas

Task One

Name five problems young people ages 18–30 have
Find two new products and two new services which might solve
one of these problems
Which is your best idea?

If possible do this with two friends

Review

Part of being innovative is an attitude of mind. Do you believe you
can find new ways to do things? I hope you realise that you can. It
is simply a question of being open to possibilities.

Let's look at a role model I encountered. One lady found that her son
had run up a £500 monthly phone bill about six months ago. She
worked in a video shop and was not a scientist. She did however have
a problem and was sensible enough to realise she was not too stupid
to solve it. She came up with a rough design of a box unit which
would block out certain numbers so that her son could not contact
them.

The solution was simple, but six months later it became available for
sale at £30 in every B&Q in UK, and the lady is set to become a substantial success story. What was so special about what she did?

She had a problem and she tried to solve it. She used simple technology and her solution was basic. However everyone who has a teenage
son or daughter is aware of the need to screen calls/websites etc. that
their children might come across. The potential market for a solution
to this problem is enormous.

It is not just the possibility that a great idea could make you or your
organisation a lot of money that is exciting. It is the realisation of the
contribution that your idea can make. For example, if you come up
with a product or service that could benefit the community, and
decide to donate it to a charity who can either raise money from it or
use it to solve problems within their target group, that is equally

innovation and creativity

enterprising. Basically in business or in life, people are continuously trying to find new solutions to old challenges. To make a difference you need to be prepared to think differently. Adopt a "what if" mindset!

So get going! One idea a day from now on.

Case Study

Let's look at a live case study. I'm sitting writing this chapter on a Sunday afternoon in May. Behind me my teenage son is sitting at his computer. He is not interested in School; he is 15 years old and shows very little motivation. My wife and I try to explain to him why he should work harder at school if he wants to have a good career.

I don't think we are getting through and neither are his teachers.

The easy answer is to give up, let him learn his own lessons. However, I am the person telling you to come up with innovative ideas, so let's look at solutions 'outside the box'.

How can I get across to him the consequences of a future with no work and no qualifications? Is there a film he can watch? Is there a teenage television programme which puts across this lesson? Who are his role models? What about a song or book or television programme that tells their story, but puts across the points that:

> Qualifications can open doors
> Hard work is essential in order to achieve anything

Can I use texting, the internet, TV his iPod or medium he already uses to get information?

The traditional answer locally is to get him to go to Church, join the Boy Scouts and do the Duke of Edinburgh Award, all of which he rejects. If he does not respond to these stereotypical solutions, what else can I do?
He has some interest in Business or Drama. Is it possible to bring this alive so that he can see what life could be like in these areas? What about inventing a computer game, or perhaps virtual reality business experience? How about setting up a competition? Use texting etc to

stay in touch. How about a business thriller written by a teenager? How about a play which he acts in which is based on a teenager starting a business? You can see that the ideas are starting to flow. I will keep you posted. If I can solve this problem, I suspect that a lot of parents throughout the world would love to know about my solution.

So watch this space. Maybe I should share the profits with you!

Is it a Process or Not?

There is a lot of argument about whether it is possible to follow a strict procedure to generate creative ideas, or whether this destroys the whole idea of creativity, which really involves making random connections and 'thinking outside the box'.

I think again it would be a mistake to exclude any method. You have to experiment to see what works for you. The most important thing is being able to produce an output of ideas that make a difference.

As mentioned earlier, being curious, doing things differently and having a notebook to record random thoughts can be a good start and it is simple (buy a little notebook today. Carry it with you everywhere, and I mean everywhere).

It would be remiss not to discuss the work of the inventor of "lateral thinking" - Edward De Bono. His view is that creativity is a process which can be taught at any level. He believes in the concept of provocation, which involves challenging traditional assumptions in any situation. "The key point about lateral thinking," he writes, "is that concepts, perceptions and structures evolve over time and are a summary of history rather than a blueprint for the future ... So we may have to cut across and break out of patterns before putting things together in a new way." Provocation is an essential part of lateral thinking, and there are various specific techniques, such as the random-word technique, which are used by de Bono to break out of this pattern-making recognition system of the brain. "The logic of provocation," de Bono writes, "shows very clearly this difference between our normal information universe and the information universe of a patterning system. In our normal universe there should be a reason for saying something. There should be a reason for making a mark in a certain place on a piece of paper. With provocation, this is not so at all."

De Bono defines provocation in the following way: "There may not be a reason for saying something until after it has been said. The point is that the provocation allows a different entry point from which different patterns emerge; the value of these patterns then justifies the provocation." Use this technique when joining a new organisation to try and observe 'the process whereby decisions are made' and then challenge.

De Bono believes that creativity is vital as all organisations need to challenge their processes, and to be proactive in seeking improvements. He devised a model 'the Six Thinking Hats,' which encourages individuals to look at problems by wearing 'different hats'; each hat representing a different perspective or 'view' of the problem. De Bono states that "In many cultures there is already a strong association between thinking and "thinking hats" or "thinking caps." The value of a hat as a symbol is that it indicates a role. People are said to be wearing a certain hat. Another advantage is that a hat can be put on or taken off with ease. A hat is also visible to everyone around". This was the reason he choose for using hats as the symbols for the directions of thinking. He provides examples of how these could be used and also emphasis that the hats are not descriptions of something that has happened but relate to the direction we should be thinking about in the future. e.g. "Let's have some white hat thinking here" means the focus should be only on information. Everyone should try and think of information that is available, information that may be needed, questions that need to be asked, or other ways of getting information, and so on; whereas when the group is asked to put on a red hat this relates to a specific request for feelings, intuition and emotions on a particular issue. Using this approach may lead to your own "eureka" moment.

Matrix Thinking™

La Salle Matrix Thinking (TM) is another recent creative thinking developments; it first emerged in the year 2000 and has rapidly been gaining momentum.

The method was developed by an Australian, Roger La Salle who is a professional engineer. Matrix thinking is both practical and applied and extremely useful for ideas generation and product development. La Salle has worked as a professional engineer in new product development for most of his life, the method of matrix thinking captures this experience in an extremely simple concept.

Essentially matrix thinking consists of a simple rectangular diagram that has so called "Seed" of thinking on the vertical axis and "catalyst", to stimulate thinking about the seeds, on the horizontal axis. In effect this diagram provides some 48 triggers for practical applied innovation and creativity.

La Salle has developed several such matrices for different applications including:

- Product Innovation
- Process Innovation
- Service Innovation
- Opportunity

He has also written two books on the subject. His web site gives further information: www.matrixthinking.com

The Disney Model

A popular model is "The Disney Model" of creativity, which specifically models the techniques devised by Walt Disney. This basically involves being as creative as possible, and suggesting any number of solutions to a problem. Then you criticise each suggestion and try to pull it apart and eventually try to pick the ideas that work best for you, that are creative but also make business sense.

As you can imagine "The Disney Model" has a big focus on letting your imagination run riot to create lots of unusual possibilities, making connections between two unrelated areas and looking for common ground.

Attitude and Mind

It is important to define goals and problems very clearly. What precisely is the problem you want to solve?

It is also important to diagnose them and to have good core beliefs like "there is always a way to sort things out". Otherwise people or companies can get too emotional about a problem, visualise the worst possible consequences, and tend to "freeze" like a rabbit in headlights even though the solution is obvious to a detached outsider.

You need to focus on times and situations where you have come up with a solution to what seemed initially to be an impossible problem.

Try to find someone – a role model who is well known for solving problems in an innovative way. Take your problem to them. Watch what they do, how they react and what processes they go through. You will probably find that they are relaxed, and firmly believe that they will solve the problem; they will often have access to some useful resources and tend to be lateral thinkers. Anyway, watch what they do and use them as models. Copy them and you should find you will achieve some degree of their success.

Groups

There is no set rule that says that you must work in groups. However, what other people do provide is a different perspective from your own. The ideal group suitable for this type of "brainstorming" an idea consists of people with diverse experience. If you have a group of say six 25 year old accountants, they may not all think in exactly the same way, but you are unlikely to bring enough diversity to solve a problem which is proving too challenging for logical analytical thinkers such as Accountants and Lawyers.

My ideal would be to create your own group of friends and co-workers who are as different as possible from each other, who meet on a regular basis to come up with new ideas/innovations. I first came across this idea when I was managing a Women's Enterprise Programme.

All of the participants on the programme had a business idea and the women all came from different backgrounds. There were Lawyers, Accountants, Artists, Housewives and Teachers. We then took the idea of one of the participants and "brainstormed". The ideas and the innovation about the ideas flowed and every participant was able to significantly improve their own ideas, and find alternative markets and methods of operation. Why did this happen? First of all there was a group dynamic where everyone seemed to perform better as part of a team. The group had been given some time to gel, and there were no major conflicts. However, the key to the success was the fact that everyone had a different perspective on the problem. The Artist was able to help the Lawyer and vice versa. This is a key to Innovation.

Everyone has a different perspective and something to offer if you are prepared to give them time and make the effort to listen to their contribution. It was amazing how the Housewife could give the computer scientist a perspective on the ways that families and children use PC's and what were the important benefits to look for.

You may well work as part of a team or have a group of friends who hang around together. If the group is comfortable together that alone is a good start.

However, also consider forming a specific 'innovation group com-prising a range of people with diverse skills and backgrounds, all of whom are aiming to produce ideas which have a commercial application.

Key features to ensure group success:-

> The building of group rapport
> Someone to lead and motivate the team
> A process within which the group likes to practice new ideas
> Some form of motivation for the best idea
> Someone in charge of follow up/implementation of an idea

It may take some time to find the right group of people but it can pay dividends.

Ideally, your group will include a person who can think laterally, a person who can share, a person who perceives the problems, and a facilitator.

There is no rule which says that groups will come up with better ideas than individuals, but try it out, get the right group dynamic and watch those ideas flow.

Tony Buzan

Tony Buzan, the inventor of mindmaps^{tm} is another person who offers ideas and solutions to boost creativity.

His focus is on thinking and the brain. He has some surprisingly simple applications however that you can apply to boost your creativity. Take breaks (I thought you might like this one!)

Fig 1.1: E Factor

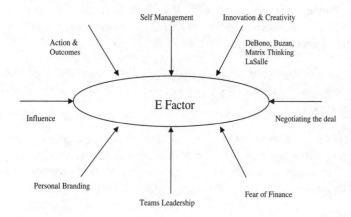

Go for long walks. Be creative in your everyday life. He believes you can bring creativity into relationships, cooking and setting a table for instance.Create your own imaginary mastermind group – a little weird perhaps. Select people who you admire as resourceful and creative. They could be business people or politicians or even historical characters. When you have got a problem ask them what you should do! I rather like this idea and as I am sharing it with you, I promise to do this for the next ninety days and then put an honest report on the Efactor website.Use Buzan's mind mapping process. This is a diagrammatic way of putting all your knowledge on an area in diagrammatic fashion.

Let me do one for you for the EFactor, starting with the title in the centre and showing a plan of this book. Here goes!

It is simply a way of arranging your creative thoughts.

Buzan does suggest you dance, sing, play music and draw.

He believes in:

Seeing things from different viewpoints
Making combinations
He also believes, as we have suggested already, that you should be curious in the same way as a child.

Conclusion

I am not saying that either Buzan or De Bono have the perfect approach. It is important to practice being creative, and if a structure helps you to do this, well and good. If not do it anyway; find what stimulates you. You may be like Archimedes and find the bath is the best place. The important thing is to have the idea. Equally important is to do something with the idea. There are no marks for bright ideas that are not acted upon. The ability to take action is another essential ingredient of the Entrepreneur which we will examine later!

Let us try to summarise what we have learned.

Yes, you are a creative powerhouse! Your only problem is that you do not realise it yet. It is a life skill from which anyone can benefit. Like all competencies, some of you will already have the skill at an unconscious competence level. That is, you are creative without thinking about it, and are recognised as a very resourceful person because you always came up with an innovative solution to any problem. However, if you have spent 20 years becoming an Engineer who practises analytical thinking, you may have some work to do to use creativity in your everyday life. I hasten to add that no one is saying you need to abandon logic, just that you can add creativity to your thinking skills to get the best possible results.

The Creativity Test

Have you ever come up with a new idea? Have you ever imagined the future? Have you ever done things differently from other people? Have you ever solved a problem you were thinking about earlier, as you drove along in the car? If so you have been creative. Have you ever challenged an assumption about the way things are normally done? You have been innovative!

It is important that you believe you can come up with new ways of doing things. It is honestly half the battle. If you are relaxed you fully expect to find a solution and because of this expectation, surprise, surprise you do just that.

Make a Commitment

Make a commitment now that for the next 90 days you will practice being creative and looking for innovation.

innovation and creativity

Be Curious and Dare to Fail

There are all sorts of people, circumstances and opportunities surrounding us every day, but we may think that we have to go to USA or the Far East to find some new innovation. The truth is a new innovation may be right in front of you. I don't know if you have ever heard the parable 'Acres of diamonds' where a man leaves home and spends his whole life searching for diamonds but dies in poverty without finding any. After his death, diamonds are found on his own ground. The moral of the story is look around you and you will find your own acre of diamonds right in your own life circumstances or contacts. Be prepared to be open and to look at opportunities that may not appear to amount to anything. As the founder of IBM said "be prepared to fail more" and you will come up with some crazy ideas and some good ideas which may lack a key ingredient that means some will be consigned to the cutting room floor.

The key thing about creativity is that if you make it part of your every-day life, you will have a consistent stream of ideas and will not be tied to the one good idea you had by chance.

Dare to be Different

The chances are that any innovation is likely to be something new and uncertain. As something new it will meet opposition since many people and organisations whatever they may profess in public do not like change.

Many of us (even those who write books about creativity and enterprise!) are creatures of habit. I find myself enjoying little routines. I like to set off for work at the same time, take the same route to the office, listen to the same radio show, park in the same space, go to the same café for breakfast and read the same newspaper. Bore of the year or what?

So I fight this. Some days I take a different route. I read a completely different news paper – in short I change my whole routine. Why? Simply, because if you keep repeating the same things in the same way all of the time, you will keep getting the same results.

That is why certain innovation experts, such as Dr John Park of Robert Gordon University in Aberdeen, worry about depending on too rigid processes/structures as ways of coming up with new ideas. The worry is that you limit your range of innovative solutions because you are again sticking too rigidly to a routine.

So go out of your way to have new experiences, travel to new places to get the stimulation you need. To innovate you must constantly look for associations or connections between products, people and markets that have no obvious link. For instance, mobile phones tend to be mainly the preserve of the young, with teenagers being particularly adapt at using all the features such as texting and ring tones. Elderly people (though not all of them) are not so comfortable with new technology, and many don't own mobile phones or shy away from using them too much.

However recently, together with a group of 300 nurses we explored new ideas during a discussion of the Health and Social Problems of the elderly. The nurses identified many different problems including difficulties in communication with the outside world, and the inability to use the simplest technology which would help significantly with safety, health and other personal and social issues. When the group brainstormed, they came up with a new mobile phone with a few basic keys for an old person, less of a toy more a simple device to meet the needs of the elderly for instant communication.

As proof that 'great minds think alike', O2 announced a week later in the press that they were designing just such a product.

Set Yourself a Daily Creativity Goal

Buy yourself a small notebook (or just use your mobile phone) and write one new idea in it every day. Carry it everywhere. The point I am trying to get across is that idea generation is not only something you do to find solutions to problems as they arise. It is something you should continually do and you will find that innovative thinking becomes part of how you view the world.
So enjoy daydreaming...

Like me, you may have been told many times to stop daydreaming. However, using your imagination, visualising situations and unusual

innovation and creativity

connections is a great way to stimulate creativity. Einstein arrived at his famous Theory of Relativity whilst imagining travelling on a time machine backwards and forwards in timelines. One proven technique that you may want to try when you have identified a goal or are facing a challenge is to visualise yourself having achieved the end result and then work backwards to identify what stages you have gone through to get that end result. Again you have "fooled" your mind that you have arrived at the end result, your subconscious will not recognise the difference and is likely to show the pathway to the end result, something that a logical planning process will have difficulty in defining.

Competitive Advantage

Unless you are lucky enough to be setting up a business, or to be employed by an organisation that has unlimited resources, you will need innovation to create a competitive advantage which will enable you to compete with the "big boys". You may not have the money to devise a traditional marketing strategy, but instead will have to adapt "guerrilla" strategies, i.e. marketing plans that can help you reach the customer without incurring the expenditure traditionally required for advertising.

So Where do Ideas Come From?

Ideas can come from anywhere. You can find an idea simply by listening respectfully to anyone. As far as I am concerned one of the most innovative businesses of recent years was 'The Big Issue'. The owner listened to the needs of many people who were trying to re-establish themselves on the work ladder to earn money independently, and funded a very successful business which also is a strong social enterprise.

Market Trends

The press and market reports will let you know major trends in your markets. What are the trends of today? A vastly increased aging population, the power of the mobile phone as a communications tool, the opening up of international trade borders, the economic growth of China and India, are obviously a few but the list is endless. There are boundless numbers of business ideas to be found simply from understanding these trends alone.

A Personal Problem

What really irritates you? Chances are it does the same to a lot of other people too. Solve it, and you have demonstrated your innovative ability.

Technology

Innovation is really about an attitude of mind which you can bring to your future work/life pursuits. However, technology is developing so rapidly that it can speed most processes up. It can also add value in many cases, but it is not always the answer. New technological processes can take several years to devise, but the simple use of basic technology to solve a problem can make a significant impact within a much shorter time period.

Different Industries

Businesses and social organisations operate differently. The way that an aeroplane manufacturer markets his product will be very different from the way financial services are marketed. The way that staff are treated in Universities may differ significantly from the way that staff in a manufacturing plant are handled, and so on. What would happen if you transferred some of the learning strategies from one industry to another? In some cases, it could transform an industry's results. For instance, Lawyers tend to adopt a fairly narrow range of marketing strategies, and many firms rely on reputations and long standing professional relationships. However, if you have a newly formed legal practice, how would you establish market share? One way could be to look at the ways in which companies operate in intensely competitive sales environments. If you adopt these strategies and customise them to ensure there is nothing contravening professional guidelines, your innovation could make a substantial and lasting impact.

innovation and creativity

Association Connection Searching

As we have discussed earlier in this chapter, it is the establishment of new connections between different areas that can produce innovation. You need to constantly search for new or simply novel connections. De Bono, Buzan and many of the other creativity gurus have created tools to stimulate connection making. For instance, there is a random word game which encourages you to take three words, build crazy connections and then take the ideas from there.

Let's do this and take three random words that occur to me now. McDonalds (I am writing this in a branch of the great 'healthfood chain'!) Pets (I was thinking of my cat, sad I know), Enterprise (I spend my life encouraging and people to be more enterprising and helping businesses be more entrepreneurial to create results). Here we go –

"McDonalds" for pets
A pet franchise organisation
Place to keep pets outside any food store
Promotion scheme for McDonalds to provide money for pet
    sanctuaries
Any pet franchises as businesses – grooming, psychology, pet
    hotels etc.
Establish pet products with a new brand name
Creativity classes for pet owners
Pet characters? For enterprise?
Use animal skills/behaviours as a way of teaching people to be
    enterprising
Marketing links between pet skills and McDonalds
A Social Enterprise to promote worldwide pet club promoted
    through McDonalds
Use the McDonalds 'child friendly marketing strategies' to
    market pets to children
Learn business skills through pet handling
Pure vegetarian McDonalds!
McDonalds staff training – Customers as pets
Pet service units set up to be as efficient as a McDonalds
Pet as new children's character to replace Ronald McDonald
Pet walking, cleaning product of business and enterprisetraining
Pet products for school enterprise projects
McDonalds pet food shops

Some very wacky ideas! I just wanted to illustrate the association process openly and honestly.

There are plenty of completely useless ideas in the list outlined above, but there are some connections to take forward. Look out for the new pet McDonalds character coming to a store near you. A week later, I have just spotted a success book based on sheepdog strategies. Weird or what?

You are likely to achieve the best results if you practice creativity on an ongoing basis and if you get other people involved who can provide different perspectives, market knowledge and who are motivated to solve a particular problem.

Without time and practice you will not improve this important E Factor. However, the enterprising person will not only be creative in thinking but will also tend to take these ideas forward. There are people who are described as great 'ideas people' who are not necessarily successful business people. However, the creation of a new idea can transform lives, and not just the life of the idea generator. Life is a constant challenge, identifying solutions which provide significant commercial or community opportunity is a worthwhile contribution to aim for. Make sure you do your bit!

What Makes a Good Idea?

Hopefully now you are a creativity powerhouse bursting with ideas (well at least you have one idea which you hope might work).

How do you know whether it is a good idea or not?

A good idea will have an obvious market, will make some use of technology, will ideally have some international potential and will be capable of being protected. It also makes life easier if your idea does not require years of research or huge finance to develop, although a cost benefit analysis of the long term market may suggest the idea is feasible.

It depends what you want from your idea, or creative thought. You may simply want to deal with a challenge which your local Help the Aged store faces, and have no interest in making a more significant contribution. However, as an enterprising person your wish to have wider impact may well lead to a greater financial reward, or to recognition for either yourself, the business you work for, or a community organisation or charity which you nominate to benefit from your innovation.

Your idea might be the greatest technical invention ever, but if no one wants it, it is likely to disappear without a trace.

If your idea can be copied and you can't protect your ownership of it, you are likely to lose it. Some ideas are 'me too' and because they lack innovative content you will lose any competitive advantage unless you can build some new way of doing things into the operation. Sadly some good ideas will also be stolen. A new invention with market potential is worth a significant sum of money, and you need to contact the patent office as soon as possible to enquire whether you can protect it.

The good news is that if you can protect it and it has market potential, there is likely to be some assistance available from outside bodies to help pay part of the cost of protection.

Trademarks, logos, designs and copyright also all provide some form of protective cover. Perhaps one of the easiest ways is to get anyone you talk to about it, to design a non-disclosure agreement before you discuss it in detail.

Having once taught a female participant on an Enterprise course for three months without ever being able to find out what her idea involved, I understand that it can be difficult to help develop some peoples' ideas. Although many people may appear to be overly protective about their ideas, it is nevertheless the case that there are some sharks out there waiting to pounce on unprotected business ideas. For example, Dyson of Vacuum cleaner fame, was forced to spend ten years fighting to protect his patent. It would be unfair to suggest that once you have a patent no one will trouble you. There are plenty of major contributories who will test your capacity and finances with a long legal fight. The realities are that the involvement of a University company or major sponsor can help with the protection.

The other reality is that getting to market as quickly as possible is almost your most effective strategy.

Commercial Help

It is important that once you have generated a new idea which you want to implement, that you do some assessment work. The first thing to do is to assess the resources you have available to make it happen. Do you have access to money market intelligence networking and to prototype and product development help? Who can provide it? You will find Regional Development Agencies very helpful here. Not only do they have staff and resources available to provide help, but they are constantly searching to promote "Global businesses". This is especially true for any product or service with international potential because of its possible economic contribution to their region.

You also need to 'self assess.' Do you have some specific commercial skills? Can you make it happen, and are you willing to develop yourself along with the product? Some business people like Sir Alan Sugar for example, seem to have not only creative capacity but also the ability to make things happen.

There are many people, without academic and technical functions, who can develop an idea, but who are very deficient in the other E Factor Skills. The whole message of this book is that you can develop your competencies in all these areas. However, while significant development is possible, if you are willing to learn and you are very creative, though lacking many of the other qualities, it can be sound business practice to either bring other Entrepreneurs into your team, or in some cases after protecting your intellectual property, to licence others to use it. If need be, you can enlist the help of independent advisers to assess your best options.

If you choose not to do this, the Innovators may change the product you make, or the business people may attempt to 'wipe your eye'. If in doubt, you should read 'the streetwise guide to starting your own business' to learn some of the business realities, to help you to make decisions and ask the right questions.

Who Owns the Idea?

If you are working for a company and you develop an innovation, be very clear who owns the rights. If in doubt, get independent advice. Many innovative contributors do not necessarily end up with the financial reward their innovations deserve; though of course many don't care. However, go into it with your eyes open!

The inventor of the Internet, one of the most significant innovations in recent years, has not achieved financial reward. There is nothing wrong with this; it depends on your motivation. Just make sure you that you get what you want as intellectual property can be very valuable.

Be Innovative or Die!

This is obviously rather a dramatic statement, but the days are long gone when either individual companies or public sector organisations could afford to 'rest on their laurels.' Constant change, global competition and continuous technological developments mean that if an organisation or an individual does not respond to these forces they are likely to be left behind.

Innovation is an attitude of mind. Even when you have a good product or service you need to focus your attention on questions such as: Does this product or service need to change to meet client needs? How can I improve my contribution to the client? What do we need to do now to take this forward?

Depending on the culture of our business or indeed the corporate structure of the place we work there will be certain 'ways of doing things' that will be encouraged. If you are, for example, a General Practitioner (GP), you are expected to follow certain procedures to protect the medical health and safety of your patient. However, this does not mean you should not be open to new ideas for treatment (perhaps suggested by your patients) or new ways of organising your surgery. If you want to lead, you should be looking to find new ways to help staff use resources and to ensure that you and your colleagues are as effective as possible.

Am I Expected to be Creative?

Obviously if you are starting a new business you will be searching for a new idea, and will need to be innovative to survive as conditions and markets constantly change. However, those of you going into professions will find that you are expected to innovate and contribute creatively. Professions and their professional bodies demand that you adapt to change.

Can I Succeed?

I have tried to tell you constantly that you can do it! The first precondition is that you should want to do it and be convinced that you can do it - otherwise you will self sabotage. Secondly, you must practice it in real life. I am about to set you a task which I want you to complete and return to me by email within the next 30 days.

Why I am doing this? It is because I passionately believe there is a big difference between knowing what to do and actually doing it. You need creativity and innovation to become a competency for you, something like driving which most of you probably do now without any conscious thought. To reach this stage, you are going to have to go through stages of practicing it, getting it wrong, getting sabotaged by others, getting to the stage of making good progress by persisting, and finally doing it as part of your range of behaviours. It will take persistence, commitment and a willingness to learn, but above all, it will require action.

It is up to you to decide whether you are happy to be aware of the growing importance of creativity and innovation, or do you want to use some of it to become more enterprising and to improve some aspect of your work life situations?

If I was your personal coach, I would be there to motivate you and cajole you everyday. If you need this help, find someone who is prepared to support you.

Although this book contains eight separate E Factors, I believe that creativity is amongst the most important. I believe that identifying opportunities and then making them happen, are the key enterprise qualities that not only any budding entrepreneur should have, but also for anyone who wants to be personally excellent in their choice of career.

I can promise you that not only will you perform better in work/enterprise, but the same qualities can also improve your personal/family life. How can you be more innovative in your relationships with children, friends, family or partner? Now it is time to complete the task. You are not allowed to move onto the next chapter, unless you email me with the task. I'm watching you!

Innovation and Creativity

THE TASK

A large American Multinational has recruited you as an "Innovation Trainer" on £50,000 per annum. You have been set the following tasks and must provide a short 500 word report to the Managing Director with your answers.

Tasks

(a) Identify 5 problems/challenges that teenagers have
(b) Come up with 3 new products and 3 services that will help them
(c) Pick your best idea and explain your reasons
(d) Outline the first four things you would do to take your idea forward
(e) Explain what you will do everyday to become a more creative person

(500 words)

Email – info@Efactor.eu

CHAPTER TWO

SELF MANAGEMENT

SELF MANAGEMENT

Introduction

Starting your own business or developing a successful corporate or community enterprise should really be straightforward. You read a "how to" manual (like the streetwise guide to starting your own business), you achieve your goals, become rich and famous and live happily ever after. Yet this rarely happens, because possibly your biggest problem will be yourself. We all know what we should do and yet we don't do it.

Why?

We all have difficulty in taking action and doing the correct thing. The ability to control our emotions and win the "inner game" with ourselves is very important. We all have a psychological make up and have been programmed by our life experience to date. Your performance in your career or business or life in general depends on your beliefs, focus, self esteem, confidence and ability to control your emotions. The question is whether you can change your make up or indeed whether you want to. The problem is that you will hold yourself back from fulfilling your full potential.

We are creatures of habit. If you have been programmed by life experiences and your family over the past twenty years have said, 'you lack confidence', or that 'you are useless at anything practical', then you begin to behave in that way. You tend to acquire very engrained habits and you tend to believe what you are told. The longer this goes on (those of you who like the author are over 35 pay attention), the more challenging it will be to break free from that mindset. It is a bit like going under the water in a swimming pool, you will have to make a tremendous effort to escape your past programming which tells you not to dive.

Can You Change?

Of course you can. People change habits all the time. They get into a different environment or find some reason strong enough to encourage them to act differently. Have you ever met a bride to be who had not slimmed before her "big day"? I have met several men with chronic smoking and exercise habits. After a stroke when their life prognosis if they don't change their habits is spelled out to them, they all underwent a remarkable change.

It is a pity though that it takes a life or death experience (I don't mean the marriage) to get us to change. What you have to do is to accept some of the principles in these cases to help bring about change. However you must actually want to change. Other people may suggest changes as good strategy but you have to want it yourself.

Interestingly, research suggests that it is easier to make big changes in your outlook or beliefs which can subsequently lead to several smaller changes.

Beliefs/Values

Your beliefs play a fundamental part in your success/performance. If you start a new project which involves a degree of uncertainty, there are plenty of people who will forecast its failure, simply because of the fact it is new and untested. You need to retain a strong belief in yourself and your project. This is a key selling point to any potential suppliers/customers/investors.

I come from Northern Ireland where people are natural pessimists. There is obviously nothing wrong with some degree of realism or preparation against unexpected events. However you will need strong self belief to help you to keep going when you meet the inevitable setbacks. The power of belief in business and support is illustrated in the recent survival of West Bromwich Albion in the Premiership football league. In the thirteen years of its existence the team at the bottom of the league at Christmas have always been relegated at the end of the season. In season 2004/5 that team was West Bromwich led by their new manager Bryan Robson. He had a well known pedigree as a great ex footballer, but had an indifferent managerial career and his team won none of their first twelve league matches. Somehow he managed to instil a belief in the team that they could survive and break all the unwritten rules.

self management

What Are Your Beliefs?

List three beliefs you have about life in general, three beliefs you have about your own ability and three you have about business.

Analyse them. Are they all positive beliefs that give you confidence and hope in everything you do, or are there some negative beliefs in there, some uncertainties which may undermine all your efforts?

I came across one client who had experienced business failure in the past. After years of relative success he became involved in a 'get rich quick' venture which was doomed to failure. He was almost "brain-washed" into believing the project would work by other associates but it failed through no fault of his own.

Samuel had always succeeded in life whenever he had worked hard either as a child or adult. This failure therefore affected him badly.

He eventually started a new business, offering business seminars - he had a talent for presentation. However whenever he recruited for a course and things started to go wrong, he literally gave up. It seemed almost as if he was looking for an excuse to bolster his new belief that "nothing ever works". This was ironic because part of his day time job involved Samuel in recruiting participants for programmes which had always been successful. Obviously this situation required urgent attention. Let me tell you some of the things we did to challenge this.

Challenge the beliefs

I spend some time with Samuel talking over the three recruitment drives for courses where he had quit. On each occasion when something went wrong his view was "I just felt it wasn't going to work out". I started to test his belief "Have you ever run a successful course?" He had! "What would happen if you kept going whatever the problems?" His response was "I might fail"! "Would that be so bad?" His response interestingly was "no". "Just because one business venture failed does that mean you will, always be a failure?" "My wife thinks so" he replied. "What do you think?" I asked. "I don't know" he replied. "What if I said you get £5,000 if you could show me you gave everything to recruit to the course whatever the result?" He smiled, "I guess I would really go for it". Why don't you take this attitude?

Visualisation

I asked him to visualise the course recruitment being successful, finding it easy to get new participants and it working out as a great success.

I told him to do this twice a day for five minutes, and to do this for thirty days. He did as he was asked, and I believe this was an important factor in boosting his belief in his ability to take action. Your subconscious mind responds to images, sounds and feelings. If you continually visualise your preferred outcome, you go a long way towards convincing yourself that it will actually happen. This is something that sports people do as part of their training routine.

Get a Set of Empowering Beliefs

No one can confirm whether a belief is true or not. People do sometimes have very strong self delusional beliefs which can lead to irrational actions. For instance there are a lot of different fundamental religious beliefs about situations where the 'believers' feel they must impose the death penalty on non believers. Not very rational!

However beliefs which inspire you can play an important part in helping you to achieve your goals.

Here are some that I have found useful. I read them every day and I am constantly looking for examples of true or fictional stories which show these beliefs to be 'true.'

There is always a way
I can make this happen
I can be whatever I want to be
There are opportunities everywhere
I love the challenge of business
I believe I can make a contribution to the world
I can be a millionaire
No matter what the problem is, I can turn it around
There is no failure only feedback
Money and opportunity are attracted to me

Obviously a track record of success helps anyone to build strong self belief. If you did well at school and played rugby for the first team you would have been considered a success, and you will believe that you will do well and will act confidently until something major happens in your life to contradict this.

Be Your Own Coach

There will be a time when the world seems to be against you. If like Samuel you lost all your money you will suffer from the vagaries of human nature. People will turn against you and will perceive you as a failure. This is not part of our culture in Britain, whereas in USA someone who has 'had a go' albeit unsuccessfully, is perceived as the type of person who will succeed provided that they learn from their mistakes.

Even one empowering belief can be useful. However it helps to have someone else who believes in you when perhaps you are at your lowest ebb and starting to doubt yourself. Samuel tried hard, but chose a poor opportunity and failed. As a result business associates, family and friends saw him as a person who was unsuccessful in business. What was ironic was that some of his 'doubters' had never actually tried any type of venture for themselves. In these circumstances unquestioned support and the ability to show belief "the past does not equal the future" are paramount for success.

We all need mentors.

Action Plan

An entire chapter of this book is devoted to being action orientated. The ability to take small action steps helps to achieve goals, but also helps to build belief as each milestone is reached. You need to tackle a situation and having established a small success, to build on that for the future.

Strong beliefs and values do help to define where you want to go.

Positive Memories

Instead of replaying in your mind situations that went wrong, remember instead when you achieved something you thought impossible. Remember the people who do believe in you. Seek out role models of people who have turned things round and achieved the impossible. What did they say? What did they do? Why did they believe in themselves?

The type of belief I want you to have is a belief in your capabilities, and able to visualise yourself achieving your goal. However I do want you to retain some flexibility particularly with regard to strategy. You may have the capabilities and the opportunity to make things happen, but there is always the possibility that your current way of operating on a project simply won't work, no matter your self confidence.

A four stage approach to being a success underpins a lot of the strategy in this chapter. Know what you want, take action, be very aware of the results you are getting; if these are unsatisfactory change your approach to make things happen.

Belief can be challenging at first because of the reactions you will get from others who are negative about new or innovative types of situations. If you have done your homework, you need self belief and a belief in your project. I have no doubt that you have excellent potential and are capable of making things happen. However you need to transmit this belief to other people, because their decision about whether to support you new venture on the basis of to two factors: The competitive advantage of the idea and your capabilities. There are lots of old clichés from the world of positive thinking, but it is true that "what you believe you can achieve".

Always believe in yourself but be prepared to learn, adapt, innovate and if necessary change course. Belief always needs to be backed up by appropriate action. If you have a vision for the long term, that will help you with your decisions along the way. It can also be useful to achieve small goals step by step, because each achievement will build your belief. This is important both for yourself and for the team you are leading.

self management

Ultimately your beliefs are a self fulfilling prophecy. To quote Henry Ford "if you believe you can, you are right. If you believe you can't, you are right. It is up to you".

Task

Develop a new positive belief that may help you to have greater impact on your ability to succeed. Do it now!

Values

It is important to know first of all what your values are and then to make sure your projects/businesses/ career are in line with those values. If you are anti nuclear weapons, it does not make a lot of sense to work for the Ministry of Defence. If the company and your values are aligned it increases the chances of successful outcomes.

> **TASK**
>
> Put the following list of values into order of preference with your most important first:
>
> >   Freedom
> >   Security
> >   Money
> >   Health
> >   Family
> >   Integrity
> >   Spirituality
>
> Give yourself five minutes to do this.

Which did you place first? There is no right or wrong answer. Is health high on your list? If security is your most important value, should you be starting a business in this age of financial uncertainty? If money is very important, are you working in a career or business that will lead to the financial success you crave? If you reordered your values, could that have a positive impact on your performance/contribution? I was reading "The Apprentice" by Sir Alan Sugar recently, based on the hit TV series, and he made it crystal clear that "Family always before business" was his number one value. Yet he seems to have done well! There are many people who put money before health or family etc. Health should be high up simply because to remain the enterprising individual you already are, you need a high level of energy and good health. When family, relationships and health are prioritised, it is less likely that there will be conflict and you can focus on achieving the task in hand.

However, you must do what you feel is right for you. Even if you achieve short term success in a lucrative venture, if the venture is contrary to your values and beliefs conflicts will inevitably arise.

Motivation

In making anything happen, the 'why' is very often more important than the 'how.' When we discuss leadership, we will look at the importance of motivating others. Entrepreneurs are essentially self starters who will do whatever it takes because of their high level of self motivation.

Your motivation will obviously be helped if you are doing what you love, are good at and when believe strongly in what you are doing. Many projects flounder but the key is to remain motivated when there seems to be a lack of immediate results or where something else intrudes.

Pain or Pleasure

People are often motivated by either pain or pleasure. They often take action when they either wish to avoid something negative happening, or where there is an obvious reward for action. Which works for you? Do both work equally well? I certainly like to earn tangible rewards, financial or otherwise for what I do. However avoidance of major pain seems to be a key driver to get me to take action.

How Do I Use This?

If you want to make a major change, let us say to become more financially successful, you know that there are strategies that will help but you frequently don't seem to get round to implementing them. For

self management

example, three key strategies which could lead to long term financial success involve buying investment property, building up a pension fund, and starting a lucrative business.

My suggestion would be as follows

Imagine yourself in twenty years time; imagine that you never got motivated and you still haven't done anything about the key financial strategies. What would your life be like? How would you feel? Imagine your lifestyle. If you visualise this in detail and turn up the pressure, you will begin to feel the pain. No money, no pension, no life, no private medical care, no money to support your family, no self respect, huge regrets and no chance to retire or make a contribution.

I'm sorry if this is quite painful, but if this is the best way to motivate yourself, we could turn the heat up.

If however reward is what motivates you, imagine the key benefits you will have if you do take action and achieve those financial goals. Imagine no work, time to indulge holidays, no worries, able to help family and friends, good healthcare, freedom to travel and go where you want.

Short Term

It is important to look at these issues on a short term basis, because the achievement of any long term goal is based on the ability to take a large number of small steps. It is important that you find your 'hot button'. What is it that will get you moving?

In selling, people will often have great difficulty in achieving a sale, because in order to get one sales interview they may have to ring ten prospects, and then have ten interviews to make one sale. In other words you may need to ring a hundred suitable prospects to get one sale. How do you motivate yourself for the ninety nine rejections along the way?

One simple solution is to work out what the value of one sale is. Let us say it is £1000. Then each of the 100 calls is worth £10. So each refusal is another £10 on the way to achieving your goal.

You need to find your 'why' in every project and use that to motivate yourself when times get tough.

It could be also useful for you to do some simple psychometric tests to help identify what it is that motivates you. Talking to family and friends will help.

People who set goals and have a mission will often have a "scrapbook" with pictures of their eventual goal, or some means of bringing this alive. Let us say what they want most of all is a lovely home in the country. Looking at the goals and the visual images once a day will help you realise why you are having all this hassle. Beliefs and values will play a part. Hyrum Smith has a test in his book on values, which asks you for whom would you be prepared to cross a plank 200 metres up in the air in order to save their life, given the likely risk of losing your own life? Your answer may surprise you. Dramatic I know, but effective!

The principle of delayed gratification is a good one. You should not always expect rewards to be immediate, and in fact you always need to have your strategic vision to hand, as the capacity to act now, for long term benefits, is something you must master. Find simple ways of relaxing yourself for action in the short term. It might be taking a bath, reading a book etc.

Control Your Emotions

We are all at the mercy of our emotions to a lesser or greater extent. Without wanting to turn you into a machine, it is important that you don't let emotions control you completely, especially in business.

Sensitivity

The right type of sensitivity is a good asset in business. Being able to read people and situations, and being sensitive to the needs of others, can be important for marketing. However being oversensitive to the opinions of others or being easily hurt will not help. We are not always able to choose what life throws at us. I do believe we ultimately determine our destiny, but we are sometimes thrown some challenges in key situations, which do not obviously appear helpful. All you can work on is your reaction to events, and try to turn them

self management

round to the advantage of yourself or others. One of the most inspirational 'one liners' I heard recently was from James Boddy, a businessman and philanthropist addressing a group of students. He told them "whatever life throws at you, get the champagne out". It is not always easy to see the joy in some scenarios which you will encounter. However you will have a better chance of working with it, if you have a positive attitude and realise it is part of your journey/test and that you must embrace it and move on with your life. I was particularly impressed by two motivational speakers I heard recently. One had had a leg and a hand blown off in Mozambique while working for a mines removal agency. His story of how he searched for his arm/leg and his relief when he realised that "he had something left, including his 'credentials', was hilarious. If he can react this way why can you not? Mark Pollack who is blind adopts the same attitude. Both men continue to physically challenge themselves and to inspire other people to face obstacles, and refuse to be beaten.

From somewhere they have got a focus we should all take when dealing with challenges. Ask yourself positive focus questions "what is good about this? What can I learn from this so I can help others? What can I do tot run this to our advantage?

Controlling State

You all know that there are certain times when we feel more 'powerful' and are more likely to achieve results. I believe that physiology plays a part. How are you standing? Are you smiling? What is your body language? Change it!

Relaxation

Your capacity to be enterprising is increased if you can learn to be relaxed. This may seem to be a direct contradiction of many small business courses. These are quite often taught by an employee of a local Enterprise agency who has never run their own business. They frequently suggest that "For the first five years of business, you must work twenty five hours a day. You can never relax!" Absolute rubbish! The first skill you must learn is to make time for relaxation. This alone will help you deal less emotionally with life's trials.

I don't know if you have ever met someone who practices meditation on a regular basis. Their very presence relaxes you. I read a profile last night of Brian Turtle, who is Director of BIFHE one of the top three Further Education Colleges in the UK. In it he explains how he enjoys his work, and doesn't worry. If he can relax with the massive financial and business challenges that he faces so can you.

The only time you are taught how to relax in this country is when you have a baby. Yet I believe relaxation is the ultimate skill for business.

Ithink we all realise that momentum is important in business. However, a relaxed focus can help an individual to concentrate on key issues, to by pass stress and to make more effective decisions.

TASK

Attend a class or find a tape teaching relaxation. It could be meditation, deep relaxation or self hypnosis. Practice for fifteen minutes every day. Also spend five minutes every day practising quick relaxation and learning to relax muscles and focus on receiving bad news.

By doing this15-20 minutes every day could change your life. It is also ideal to be in a relaxed state should you want to visualise the achievement of future goals, or habit change. Being relaxed helps you visualise with your 'right brain' and stops the incessant analysis and chatter which gets in the way.

Fears

We are frequently driven by our fears, and although you can't get rid of them completely, you must not let them get in the way of goals. It is reasonable to be afraid of dangerous animals, dangerous road conditions and serious illness. What you have to work on are the irrational fears that hold you back. If we are afraid of something, our natural reaction is to avoid whatever is causing the fear. People become so skilled at this avoidance that they may end up keeping away from some of the important things in life such as relationships.

self management

Irrational fears can be very extreme after some particularly bad experiences and can almost turn into a "phobia". If you have a fear this extreme, you may need to get some professional help.

However you can improve your ability to cope with fears through a number of approaches. Find out what works for you.

Fear Will Always Be There

A lot of approaches get us to accept that the fear is not going away, to accept it but to go ahead and do what you have to do. A lot of seminar leaders will get you to do something you never thought possible, like walking on fire. Having found that under the right conditions this was possible to do, then you should be able to let go of your fears.

Have You Any?

Do you have any underlying fears that could hold you back? At least admit it to yourself. A few of the key fears that hold you back in enterprise are fear of having to take risks, fear of failure, and fear of rejection. Statistics show these are very significant fears which tend to inhibit many peoples' ability to take action.

You will need to work with this fear if you are going to achieve any significant success. We will discuss this further when we look at personal influence. You will face rejections even when you are only asking for people to help you. If you take these no's personally you will quickly become inhibited. Searching for team members, looking for help, and selling are all examples where not everything you do will work. As Watson of IBM advised "you need to fail more often".

School does not prepare us for failure, and yet that is how you will learn not only in sales but at every stage of any project. You do not know who is going to help, who is going to hinder and who is going to help you achieve results.

This means that you have to be relaxed about both rejection and failure. In bringing any innovation to life there will be plenty of both. This is where someone who has some type of direct sales experience has an advantage, because this is one activity that teaches you to be relaxed about the fact that not every one will support you or everyone will agree to your requests.

Geoff Thompson who was an ex Martial Arts specialist before becoming an author and a playwright, used his own version of "systematic desensitisation" where he grades his fears, and gradually works his way through them achieving success at every step.

If you are afraid to make a presentation to the board of directors of a company for instance, presenting to a friend and then perhaps a small presentation to a group of colleagues may help by gradually reaching a more challenging audience until you are ready for the board. Sometimes you may be ready to "jump in at the deep end" and although this type of approach can be very successful, you have to be prepared for it to go wrong and to learn from it.

Geoff Thompson's greatest fear was physical confrontation. To overcome this he became a nightclub bouncer which forced him to deal with, and overcome his fear. However I don't think you will need to do anything quite so drastic!

If you have identified what is the real fear that is holding you back you are halfway there. Work on your fear, tackle it step by step. Every attempt no matter how small is a major step forward.

In my youth I had a very severe fear of speaking in public, after participating in a particularly unsuccessful "mock court debate" during my first year at University. I spent about three years successfully avoiding speaking in front of a group again. Suddenly I was asked to take a 'one off' class at a Further Education College. I had no choice but was not happy. However the girls in the class, who were final year A level students were friendly and quite undemanding. I started to believe that I could do it and today speaking to an audience holds no fears for me. If an idiot like me can do it, so can anyone!

Confidence and Self Esteem

You need to learn to like yourself. Once again it comes down to programming. If you lack confidence it is not because you were born that way, it has a lot to do with our environment. Many of us come from well meaning families who do not want us to 'get above ourselves' as children. This can lead to a lack of confidence in our own ability. You need to realise that you have talents and you have every right to be confident in doing anything which you have experience of

self management

or which reflects your personal abilities. Affirmations can prove useful. "I like myself" is a very simple one but effective. "I can and I will" are examples of affirmations that should be repeated on an ongoing basis.

One useful ploy when carrying out a task that you do not feel confident about is to act as if you are totally confident. This will help you to act differently and to get a reaction from your audience. The ironic thing is by moving differently, acting out our role and achieving at least some success, will mean that we start to feel more confident.

It is always nice to have some cheerleaders in your life. I don't mean that in a literal sense! I am thinking of people who will encourage you. You need to be careful about whom you share your hopes and dreams with; it could be a member of your family, a friend or a mentor at work.

Visualisation can also be a useful strategy. In your daily relaxation session imagine yourself as being totally confident, acting confidently and being the person you want to be. If you can do this for five minutes every day your confidence levels will sore.

You will also have to monitor your 'self talk.' If you have this little voice inside your head which tells you every time you do something wrong that "you are useless", you need to change that.

Simply change your focus to "how can I do better next time?"

Learn to respect yourself, treat yourself just as you would a friend you were trying to encourage and help to develop. Not only do you have to master communication with the outside world, you have to work on it yourself.

Be careful of the words you use. Let us say you have forgotten to tax your car. To say "this is a nightmare" is an inappropriate use of language. Work on what memories you want to enhance and what you want to forget. Try to remember an occasion when you were a big success.

Imagine this is happening again. Recreate the sounds and the feelings to produce a positive association. If you have had an experience which haunts you and effects your confidence, see it as a distant picture with yourself in it, keep the image dull and lifeless and free of any emotion. This will help to prevent the habit we all tend to have of reliving bad memories.

A final strategy can be to remember a time when you acted confidently and felt good. Find something visual or a piece of music which you associate with that occasion. Anytime you want to recapture that feeling, find something visual, some sound or some feeling which will bring it back to life.

TASK

Think of a time when you were very confident and felt at your best. Turn the sound up; remember what you saw and what you felt. At the peak of the memory touch your thumb and forefinger together. Do the same thing five times. What do you notice?

Work on yourself and be careful about the messages you give yourself. You may have spent years being "modest", thinking that this was the way to behave. However confidence is an essential part of your enterprise package. People will respond well to confidence but not to arrogance. It is possible to treat people with consideration and still be quietly confident.

You need to gradually do more things and learn to be relaxed about the outcomes. If you are prepared to take action, relax and learn from your experiences you have every right to be confident. Confidence should be based on the ability to 'have a go', rather than on trying to be someone who never makes mistakes. The attitude you need to foster is "Whatever happens I can turn this around" or "I can make this happen". Other people are attracted to confidence and are more likely to support you if you are confident. Be as confident as you possibly can. Remember that you are only using a small part of your talents/capabilities/brain. Are you interested? Are you prepared to learn? If the answer to these two questions is yes, then be confident.

self management

Time Management

You will have to challenge any habits which reduce your personal effectiveness. Your ability to make use of your time is crucial. A friend sent me a visual representation of the fact that there are only have 86,400 seconds in a day and that time is the one resource which gets scarcer every day. In that time you want to be successful in your career/business and to lead a happy and fulfilling life. Quite often you will feel that there really only seems to be enough time to focus on one or other of these ambitions.

Nevertheless we have to work within this valuable resource and to get ourselves the best deal possible.

Pareto's law applies clearly here. 20% of your time will produce 80% of the results you are looking to achieve, so you need to identify and focus on your key priority tasks.

Sometimes the 20% can be the most difficult tasks, but if you can personally deal with these, you might be able to delegate the other 80%. You need to share your time between things that are urgent now, and things that are important. This is difficult, and something that those of you who have your own business will struggle with. There are always so many loose ends to tie up, and decisions which need to be taken in order to keep the momentum of your project going. However the strategic use of part of your time can mean that less time will be needed to 'fire fight' in the long run.

The 'power of now' is a good philosophy to adopt in the use of your time. If you are at   work, focus on that the whole time. Do not take long lunch breaks or socialise too much. At the same time when you have blocked out your family or recreational time do not let other things intrude. That is what high performers in business do if they are also to be people who enjoy a happy family and personal life. I know we do advocate working on things you love, but some people use this as an excuse to make work everything, to always be at the office and to never really leave it mentally when they come home. If Richard Branson and Alan Sugar always take weekends off surely you can do the same.

Ability to say No

Linked to your ability to assert yourself, you should learn to say 'no' to activities, you are not good at or which intrude on your time.

Managing Several Tasks

If like me, you are involved in several projects, it can be difficult to know where to start and where to finish. The key again is to set time aside for each task and focus exclusively on that task. You must always build in a degree of flexibility however, in order to cope with the unexpected things which invariably intrude.

Time Management System

It is helpful to have some type of time management system, either manual or computerised. Plan your time ahead with a degree of flexibility. Again, use the power of leverage to achieve results through the use of other peoples' time. If all you do is sell your own time there is a limit to what you can achieve financially or otherwise.

Chunking

In project planning it is a good idea to set a timetable and 'chunk down' things into individual bits. As one commentator said "how do you eat an elephant?" answer "a bit at a time".

At the start of each day you need to ask yourself "what can I do today to move my life forward", and at the end of each day you should ask yourself the question "what did I do today? What contributions did I make?"

There can be a tendency to rule out community activities on the basis that there will be plenty of time later for that when you retire. However you do not know how long you have got, so making a contribution without looking for a return can add immeasurably to your life and give you a different perspective on life. I was particularly taken by a social enterprise which was set up by a church in my own area. They have created a modern trendy café from which all profits go to helping third world enterprises. Additionally the church has an

self management

ongoing commitment to running community activities at the café as part of the ethos of the enterprise.

Relaxed Focus Momentum

Time taken to relax (remember your fifteen minutes every day) is also time well spent. It will improve your creativity and reduce your stress levels. Spending time relaxing and taking exercise are very strategic, as bad health can undermine all your activity. No matter how efficient you are there is always room for improvement.

Momentum

As well as your "timeouts" it is important to live every day as if it must not be wasted. An example could be to think about how you would use your time if you were told that if you were able to clear your work up over the next few days, a helicopter would be coming to take you to Acapulco. Would it concentrate your mind? Sadly many of us only tend to work that way when we have urgent deadlines. We may enjoy the adrenalin rush but the sad thing is that this means that we normally waste a lot of our time.

TASK

Keep a time log for a week, and work out where you spend a lot of your time. Is there anything you would like to change? How much time are you spending on strategic long term issues?

Time moves on and you can't go back. Make sure you are spending time on what is important for you. I am the one who is showing you how to be more enterprising. However it should not be at the expense of the rest of your life.

My belief is that an enterprising person values time and makes the best use of it. You have heard the old adage, "give a busy man something to do." Some people get through so much in a day in all aspects of their life. Others never seem to have time for anything.

Time is a resource, possibly the ultimate resource; you need to value it in all aspects of your life. Don't follow the example of the author who once paid £150 for a time management course, but found that he did not have the time to go to it.

There are no magical systems, but find one which works for you, especially if one of your aims is to make the best use of your time now, so that your business and family will both benefit in the long run. I frequently see examples of people who have got the time equation wrong – successful business men in their 70s who are still working 60hrs per week, or bored pensioners who retire early and without the value of work, fill their time by watching soaps on the TV.

There is a tendency to live each day the same and think that you have as much time as possible. Having lost a very close relative recently whom I rarely managed to see because I was too busy, I often wish I could go back and change how I spent that time. However as Omar Khayyam the ancient Tibetan poet said, "The moving finger writes and having writ moves on". "Nor all their piety nor all thy wit shall change a single word of it". Food for thought!

> **TASK**
>
> Which two things could you change now to make the best use of your time?

Health

I am the last person to lecture anyone about health. I do realise that most high performers must have a lot of energy to achieve what they do. You need to watch diet and exercise. Take fifteen minutes of exercise four times a week, make sure your diet is relatively low in carbohydrates and fat, and your ongoing relaxation will all help with stress. There is an optimal level where you can enjoy stress, but beyond a certain point it can cause difficulties. For example high blood pressure is something which should be monitored. Regular health checks are also important. There is a tendency only to get there when suddenly we don't feel well, but pro-activity is what matters.

self management

For those of you who are at the early stage of your career it may be difficult for you to take health habits too seriously. However although bad habits may not affect you now, those habits will be difficult to shift later on.

Strategic

Try to look at both long term and short term aspects of anything you are working on. A friend of mine was saying the other day that she had noticed in middle age that the people who had knuckled down to get qualifications or experience early on were reaping the dividends in career terms now.

Unfortunately even public sector organisations now have performance measured by short term budgetary performance criteria. Is there anything you can spend time on now, which will help you in the long run?

Personal Development

The focus of this chapter is on trying to help you to develop your potential and to challenge 'the enemy within'. Unfortunately we all have aspects of our personality that we would like to change. There are many people who think that personal development is "bunkum" and who want to ignore it. There are others who attend every personal development course available, and who tend to build their favourite authors/speakers into guru status, convinced that by attending the courses they will eventually get 'the secret'.

There are many factors that have made each of us into the person we are. To have any hope of change, firstly you must want to change. Secondly you have to accept that you will not change overnight but that you are on a journey – though at times it will seem very like one step forward and one step back.

It is particularly frustrating if you are acquiring knowledge about how to change and want to share it with others but never get round to doing it yourself. The most effective teaching is not delivering a lecture but being a model for someone else, because you then have integrity and do what you say you are going to do.

The key to personal mastery is the ability to be 'self aware' and to seek feedback from people you trust. The annoying thing (tell me about it) is that it is much easier to help other people change, than to do it yourself. Accept that you are human and although you will not always 'walk your talk' you will do your best.

There is no single system that works for everyone. You will come across people who will advocate positive thinking, therapy, or the works of one particular guru. However there are no set answers and basically all of these models teach the same basic principle. Relax, visualise, and build your self esteem. Learn to control your emotions and take action. There is no set length of time that this will take. However do prepare a personal development plan.

TASK

What aspect of your behaviour would you like to change now? Work on it! Some changes will be easier to make than others, however even small changes can make a big difference. The premise of this book is that you are only as strong as your weakest area. Work on it, improve it a little, and you will leverage the effect on your life as a whole.

Be in control of your own development, and know not only where you want to end up but what type of person you will become as a result. Success can be just as much of a challenge as failure. Are you still your same old self? As you develop on the E Factor and move forward, even though you are already a multimillionaire, a success in conventional terms, don't change! Underneath you are still the same person who respects other people and will never 'sell out' to the establishment. Let us say 'Develop and remain the same'. Quite a challenge!

---

self management

CHAPTER THREE

NEGOTIATING THE DEAL

NEGOTIATING THE DEAL

I believe there are two core competencies which characterise enterprise (E Factor) – an individual's level of assertiveness and their power of negotiation.

I do however have a confession to make, like everyone some of my E Factor scores are better than others.

I have been proactive and generally good at goal achievement and have even been accused of being "pushy" in the past. However, I am not naturally very good at dealing with aggression, I avoid confrontation and will not always speak up as I should. I am also not very good at saying no. These are all areas that I have had to work on. The whole point of the E Factor is to work on all areas which contribute to the two core competencies but particularly focus on any weaknesses which may block your progress. I have found to my cost several times in business that "niceness" can be perceived as weakness.

You have to find your own communication style that works but it is something I practice every day. I keep a journal and record every day my victories and defeats.

Assertion is therefore one of the 20% of activities that will make 80% of difference in my activities. When I am ready I am looking forward to in particular leading   assertion classes. In other areas such as finance or creativity I have developed the skills but assertion is an area where I have been like a recovering alcoholic and may be able to contribute more in the future. Through personal experience I now have a greater understanding of what motivates others and use their perspective to guide my behaviour towards them. This will allow me to see the world through their eyes and alter my approach (and level of assertiveness) to achieve the desired outcome.

Now read on!

So What Is Assertion?

Assertion is standing up for your rights without hurting anyone else. Aggression is where you are prepared to "walk over the top" of someone else to get what you want. Timidity is where you do not stand up for your rights and let others do whatever they want. People often confuse aggression with assertion.

You will find a lot of aggressive people in business and therefore the myth is perpetuated that this is the way you must be to succeed in business. People who do not find this a natural way to behave however often find themselves following this model rather than pursuing the route of assertiveness.

If you do pursue the aggressive route and do not consider the rights of other people and are overly aggressive do not expect to deal with that person or business a second time. You may be met with opposition straight away or even if you have won a victory there is a cost. The ideal model has got to be "win win" where you try if possible to create a deal where both sides gain from the deal.

However, let's be honest, it is better to be aggressive than to be too nice and to let other people always have the upper hand. It is an unfortunate aspect of human nature that people will often take advantage of nice people. I'm sure you have offered help or advice at no cost to someone else only to see them take the credit publicly with no sense of shame or embarrassment.

What you will find is that your style of communication will vary with the different groups you communicate with. This is due to the situations we find ourselves in and it often has more effect than our own personal style. For instance, an aggressive manager at work may be lacking assertion at home with his children indulging their every whim through guilt for spending too much time working. Often business leaders who are extremely competitive find themselves with little time for home life. The assertive schoolteacher may have no problem at school but be unable to assert themselves in home or social settings.

Why are we assertive/aggressive?

Again our programming and out environment has played a part. Sometimes as parents we want our children to be obedient and do what they are told. School rules can also follow the same format. This can lead the model child to become a "yes man" as an adult and to have difficulty with authority figures. Again it is a learned behaviour.

negotiating the deal

However to be successful in business individuals need to learn how to act independently and be proactive in seeking solutions.

Aggression appears to be increasing in our culture. The problem with being too nice is that avoiding conflict and keeping the peace can lead to resentment and potential aggression in the long run.

You need to learn to say no. For some politeness has been a taught behaviour and generally goes hand in hand with always saying yes. However you must learn to stand up for yourself if you want to have any chance of getting what you want. That is what negotiation is about. Life consists of a series of deals with family, friends and business contacts. If you constantly take less than 5% of every deal you do not get what you deserve. The danger is this can become a serious liability. What I hope my suggestions will do is provide you with a framework to practice the middle ground behaviour.

When you are a child your parents or even big brothers/sisters are there to stick up for you. When you are an adult you have to do this for yourself. What you earn, how your life and business runs depends to a degree on how well you do this. Other people will tread on your toes and try to take advantage sometimes without fully intending to. If you do not let them know directly that you are not happy with a situation be sure the situation will only get worse. Sometimes non assertive people will still want their way and will try to do it indirectly. They will manipulate and cajole and can be seen as devious because they are not upfront with their feelings/thoughts. Although honest communication is desirable some form of subtlety is at times required. People generally feel comfortable dealing with someone who they feel is consistent. If they make a deal whatever the terms, they like to think that both parties will stick to it.

ASSERTION TASK

Here is an assertion checklist. Please tick the areas you have problems with. Those of you who are much too aggressive are likely to have the most difficulty in recognising you have a problem because after all you are never wrong!

Select as many as appropriate

> I can never say no
> I hate confrontation
> I am too aggressive
> I want to be liked
> I hate rejection
> I don't like speaking up
> I will put up with a lot
> I put myself down
> I find it difficult to cope with other people's aggression
> I don't like to make a fuss

If you have ticked (1–3) of the areas you have work to do. If you choose all of them you will need to develop an assertion plan. If none of them, congratulations. If you are not sure get feedback from others you can trust. People with assertion problems either believe they can't stand up for themselves at all or are blissfully unaware they have a problem, and take pride in their aggression.

The best communicator is the most flexible. If you want to build rapport with the other side in a negotiation, sometimes a more laid back but firm style will work, sometimes you need to show the same level of assertion but adopt a strong approach.

Everyday Life

The beauty of assertion is that you can practice it in every day life. You maybe want to build up to asking your boss for a raise or need to deal with a difficult workmate. Start off with much simpler tasks i.e., sending food back in a restaurant when you are unhappy with the dish, or saying no to someone who is trying to sell something in the street. I think I have got too good at this skill as street sellers rarely approach me.

Small victories and defeats matter. Record them and learn what you did wrong.

Rehearsal

If you have for instance an interview presentation or a difficult meeting coming up; it can be useful to role-play with a friend. Do this a couple of times and you will be better in the real situation.

Body language/Tonality

In putting your point across it is important that you are congruent. As you know words only convey 5% of the meaning. The other 95% will be conveyed by tonality and body language. You may manage to say "no" but the full communication must show that you mean business; that you mean what you say. Again you will have practice getting this "congruency" across. If you will carry out role-plays and rehearsals these will all help however, there is nothing to beat a real life situation. It may only be telling your friends you can't put them up on Saturday night. Obviously this is not quite the same as having to confront your business partner about an irregularity in the accounts but it is a start.

What is important is doing the work that will eventually lead to a situation where you feel comfortable and confident is saying what you feel no matter who you are dealing with.

Some of you may be assertive in many areas but fail miserably in one or two other areas, which potentially may create real problems for you.

Is this an issue for females only?

Assertiveness is quite often taught in women's personal development courses however, it is a problem which exists for both males and females.

> **TASK**
>
> Identify the situations/ types of people where you may have difficulty being assertive.
>
> Which are the most critical? Choose one to work on intensively.

It is important you do understand how you came to be the way you are and in which situations it is a liability. I also want you to feel you can make a choice and take action.

Are you wrong being too nice?

To be agreeable, helpful or considerate will often be perceived by others in a positive light. For those of you who are too aggressive and wonder why you get people's backs up, you can learn a lot for this approach. Some people will try to help others by offering solutions and generally being agreeable. However, it is not always appropriate in business to be 'too nice', particularly when you are trying to demonstrate that you mean business.

What type of situations can this include? For instance, if someone is trying to "walk over the top of you", is insulting you or your work then there is a need to be more direct. If you feel powerless in this type of situation, that is definitely a liability. You need to realise, if you are always too nice people they get fed up with your indecision. They also may consider you "too nice to be wholesome". Someone recently who would ask my opinion on their work performance got a little fed up when I gave my usual "nice" response of "you're doing really well" responding with, "you never give an honest opinion".

Should everyone like you?

It is unlikely that everyone will like you. Some people will dislike you without even knowing you and it can be a shock for us "people players". I remember as a graduate entrant in National Westminster Bank being put into a local branch to "learn the trade" being hated for being a graduate on an accelerated scheme, and for being Irish. The answer was to be relaxed, focus on work performance accepting that people will take time to get to know the real you.

TASK

Your boss has given you a report to finish. You are really struggling and are not going to meet the deadline. Should you talk to him?

Answer

The passive person is likely to think of the worst consequences and be scared of what is going to happen if they are not going to make the deadline. You are coming up with your own rules, 'shoulds' and 'musts'. You should talk to him having decided what outcome you want from the meeting i.e. the need for more time, information or resources in order to finish the report, making sure you provide a reasonable argument as to why it cannot be finished on time.

Telling the people

There are a few people who are genuinely nice all the time but many people feel anger; they want to confront the person who has caused it, but instead they talk to third parties. Why? Sometimes they can be scared of triggering off somebody's anger. It can be shocking to realise that other people do not have the same map of the world as you; they don't worry about offending people by saying what they think. People do not have to conform to your expectations and way of behaviour. The only person's behaviour you can change is your own. It is important that you act as you feel, and are not perceived on the outside as a person with no opinions and who is always nice but inwardly seething about everything. It is bad for your health, and self esteem.

Why am I that way?

You were certainly not born passive. Babies are naturally assertive to get their needs met. It is likely that it came from your environment particularly from your family. My mother god rest her soul was a very good and kind individual. Like all parents there is no training that goes with the job – we do the best we can. My father was very bad tempered and although he was less bad tempered with at least one of my sisters, he did not accept 'answering back'. The first time I answered my father back was at the age of twenty. As a result when people in authority or aggressive people try to bulldoze me into doing things I shouldn't do, my natural inclination is to say yes to please them. This is an example of twenty years of programming. New behaviour has to be practiced to become established.

> **TASK**
>
> Is there anything in your childhood, family/school situation that could explain some of your assertive hang ups?

Fear of Consequences

Your imagination can run riot. If I tell this customer I can't do this work they will get angry then they will go elsewhere. It is true that sometimes people will react as you anticipate. The problem for you is you imagine it is going to happen every time rather than just some of the time.

The fight or flight syndrome

These are two primitive responses which are in us all. Fight is the primitive response where you get ready to defend yourself. Flight can mean you continually walk away from a situation where there could be a confrontation. Again sometimes it can be good to get a clear head, however sometimes you may be making things worse.

It is sometimes difficult to control our physiological response to these feelings. What you need to do is change your focus response from a 'sick feeling in your stomach' when you want to stand up for yourself, to asking yourself 'how can I take action here'?

negotiating the deal

Anger

We all feel anger some time or other. Do you explode or implode? Neither is particularly good and yet anger is a natural emotion.

The problem is if you are nice when you should be assertive, you are going to be put upon. If this goes on too long you will go straight to "nasty temper". This approach usually leads to an even greater mess

Could your behaviour be generally described as 'like going up and down the gears of a car'? You are either in first or fifth and never in between. You should be able to change your speed to suit the road conditions. You need to change your behaviour to suit the type of person and situation you face. If your child is in physical danger that is not the time for passive Mr Nice. People may not be deliberately trying to hurt you when they need something done, but in getting something done people will look for the most accommodating route. Start to be aware if you are giving off any signals which say "choose me". Look to make small changes that give you a better chance of operating effectively.

It's all a game

To change your behaviour to improve any of the E Factors you need to practice. The first time you use any of the strategies it will probably not work. However enjoy it; it is a game which through practice you will become more likely to win more often.

What is difficult about adopting a more assertion stance is that once you start to use some of the strategies you will also come up against resistance from others. Your friends and family who are used to taking advantage of you may not initially like or understand the new you.

Watch your language

Those who are generally less assertive tend to use particular types of words. Don't over apologise, using phrases such as, "I'm so sorry to ask you this", often this dilutes the message you are trying to give. Start to observe both the internal chat in your head and how you speak to others.

Stop!

Every time you tell yourself off say to yourself stop! Ask yourself the question, "how can I prove myself here?"

> **TASK**
>
> Next time you catch yourself apologising for nothing or using passive language say "stop!"

Strategies

Certain things are important when you are being assertive, maintaining eye contact, not smiling too much, not getting drawn into a conversation and keeping the conversation as short as possible.

The Status Quo

In work or within a business there always seems to be a pecking order. People tend to treat people according to their status and power. You will alter your behaviour depending on who you are with. Quite often you will vary your body language, tonality and words.

Where appropriate you have to act to raise your status.

    Someone with high status
        takes their time
        uses silence
        listens without comment
        maintains eye contact

You can also lower your status for effect.

Let us say you have a friend who earns less than you and has got used to you helping them out e.g. with money. If they are constantly trying to manipulate you to lower your status, play them at their own game, use sympathy, show you support their position and wish you could help if only you can afford it.

negotiating the deal

Play the numbers

Always remember you have a choice to play, 10 (high status) or 1 (low status).

It is important to sometimes change the status level to be assertive in the appropriate situation. Using this model you may get it wrong a few times but you will learn.

Don't rise to the bait

People have learned what buttons to press to manipulate you. Have fun learning how to avoid them.

Practice

Deliberately have nice days when you are sweetness and light and not so nice days where you are more direct and forthright. Observe the effects of your behaviour and learn from it.

Look for any opportunity no matter how small to practice the skills.

There is no need to change your personality or try to be become someone or something you are not. Remain "nice" but someone nice with an edge who can adapt to circumstances and different people and communicate effectively.

I cannot emphasise enough how effective some of these exercises will be if you practice often. People trying to encourage enterprise spend a lot of money giving people help on business fundamentals and on completing their business plan. However they need to realise this help will go to waste if the budding entrepreneur is unable to be assertive. Let me show you the areas where a lack of assertion can count against the enterprising person.

> Being given a poor deal by their bank manager
> Being bullied by suppliers and customers
> Customers taking too long to pay
> Paying too much for everything
> Conflict with partners
> Breaching ethical rules to please customers

Being too aggressive to everyone
Being bullied by government agencies

The list goes on; in business you will come across aggressive business people who will try to win at any cost. Government agencies who will bully you, difficult customers, suppliers and staff who will try to impose their rules on you; you will need to stand up for your business or you will not survive. You will need to be assertive with professional advisers who only agree with your own views rather than offer their professional opinion.

Negotiation

Negotiation is a process and has some similarity to sales which is covered in personal influence. Sales is really one type of negotiation, as you make deals in every aspect of your business. In doing the deal you need to assert your rights otherwise you will get a poor deal, lose money or lose ground.

I have found it to be a core business and life skill, and yet again something which is not taught in the academic curriculum.

"Everything is Negotiable"

Gavin Kennedy an Edinburgh Professor wrote a book with this title. It is a good mindset. We can all believe in fixed procedures, set rules or set prices, but they should be challenged.

There is no set price

There are no set prices. Some of us love to haggle naturally for others it is an embarrassment. However if you don't ask you don't get. It all depends on the deal. Suppliers may be prepared to reduce the price of product if there are other certainties/favourable points built into the deal.

The Art of the Deal

This is the name of a book written by Donald Trump who spends most of his life putting together property deals. It is more of an art than a science. You need to learn to find your own style that works

negotiating the deal

for you. The traditional negotiation model is of "playing aggressive hardball". However that may not be suitable in the circumstances or not be your style.

Do your homework

As with sales you need to prepare before the deal. You need your technical data and you need to know the personalities and what are their key objectives.

You will also learn a lot face to face during the negotiation. You will sense how much the other party wants to deal and on that basis can decide your own strategy.

The deals you make are the life you make

Your career/enterprise is very dependent on your deal making capabilities. Your relationships are also a deal, and you have got to strike a fair compromise.

It is very easy to get the deal wrong. If a key condition or pricing structure is left out, the whole deal can fail.

Decide what you want

You need to know what outcomes you must have, and what are desirable as you may be required to trade something.

Rapport and understanding

It is important to build some sort of rapport. You need to spend time getting to know each other and your positions. You are unlikely to agree with the other side's perspective, but it is useful to seek to understand it and to try if possible to be "win win". If you try to get everything you create bad relationship, no further deals and a reputation as someone who has to take everything in the deal. There is strategic value in giving the other side something.

Decide where to start and where to end

If you start off by stating exactly what you want you will end up getting less. People will usually pitch lower until they see the position.

Be prepared to walk away

It will always be to your advantage if you are genuinely prepared to walk away if the deal is not right. The other party will remember this and it will strengthen your position.

Get the deal in writing

A lot of older business people like to think when they have shook on a deal that the transaction is sacrosanct – you always need a written signed contract to spell things out, in the event of any future dispute.

Don't take things personally

Things may be said during a negotiation that can normally lead to offence being taken. A negotiation is no time to be too sensitive and your ability to remain relaxed but focused on the outcome is critical.

Creativity

A negotiation is not a time to stick to one position only. You may have fall back positions but your challenge is to sometimes find a lateral position particularly where there is deadlock.

Who has the leverage?

Who has the strongest position? If it is you make sure you use whatever leverage you can use. If the other party has it, giving up is not the best option. The best negotiators even if in a weak position can sometimes make the positions seem more balanced simply because of their position. I remember a small business client who had a £30,000 unsecured overdraft and was therefore in serious trouble berating his Bank Manager for not looking after her properly. If you refer to the orientation material you need to adopt appropriate status behaviour.

Review their perceptual position

People do see things differently. Your ability to see things from other people's perceptual position is important.

> **TASK**
>
> Take time out. Think of a situation where you are at log-
> gerheads with someone else. Imagine you are the other
> person, what are you thinking? What do you want out of
> the negotiation? Change and become a third person not
> involved in the deal. How do you see it sitting on the out-
> side, what do both parties want? How can you help?

Do not accept their first offer

This is the worst thing to do. Not only is it likely to be their "worst
offer" but the other party will expect you to haggle. In fact by accepting someone's first offer you will make them worried that they have
got it wrong.

I can't emphasise that once the first offer is made, that is when the
dealing is done. For instance at one stage of my career I got a job I
really wanted and needed. I wasn't particularly happy with the payment but immediately accepted thinking I would easily up my package once I was in the organisation. I found to my dismay that this was
not how it worked. The time to sort out the deal was at the beginning.

Look for tradeoffs

If you have a grievance, focus on getting something more from the
deal.

What if?

This is your key question to ask when making the deal. It is too late
to ask afterwards. You have to get answers to all sorts of contingen-
cies and change the deal to reflect it.

Learn to enjoy it

Research I have carried out on top negotiations show that they love
to deal. It may not come naturally to you and you may find it embar-
rassing initially; rest assured if you don't or won't negotiate you will
get much less out of life financially or otherwise.

You need to learn to enjoy it. Negotiation is a game and you can simply get better by playing the game. Let us say you are getting a new cleaner for your house. Practice deal making, make sure you get a fair deal. Work up to where you could negotiate with your bank manager or boss at work.

Reputation

Work on your business reputation. Deals will be much easier for you if you have the right reputation "hard but fair" is the type of reputation you want. The reputation of "very easy to deal with" can leave you with a reputation as a pushover. If you constantly make deals and then don't stick to them this will run your credibility in negotiations.

How do you get this reputation? Two ways:

> How you have handled previous negotiations
> PR

We talk in the book about your personal branding. It is important to think through how you present yourself as that is how you are perceived.

The Details

All details matter. This can include everything from what you wear to where the venue is. This should all be included in your planning. However details will emerge which may change the structure of the deal. Be prepared to use that to your advantage.

TASK

Go out and search for a consumer item such as a new TV. Use this situation as a chance to negotiate a deal. Unless you want to buy it at the end of the negotiation say you will go back and think about it. Practice your skills. It is preferable if it is something you want, but there is no practice like the real thing.

What did you learn?

Review

What we need you to overcome is the embarrassment of asking for a reduction or a change in a deal, particularly when the other side like to make you believe that the terms are fixed. When you make someone a really low offer for something with a high mark up they will be shocked and possibly initially angry.

You hear people using the phrase " I won't insult you with a silly offer". Good business people are not afraid to make low offers, particularly if they are used to buying and selling. They believe that you can make an offer as low as you like, and sell as high as they like.

One author recommends you go into an electrical goods shop where you see a TV priced say for £500. Walk up to the salesman and offer him £30 just to get used to the reaction.

I am not recommending that you always aim to take advantage of people but you must get used to the fact that in many cases people will value their products, services and assets much greater than you do. Unless your aim is to get people to like you, constantly pay over the odds and lose money, you are going to have to negotiate.

There may be occasions when you bring someone in to negotiate on your behalf, but it is not practical to do so all the time. As life is a series of deals the ability to negotiate is key.

Posture

It is important that you get your posture right. Opponents are looking for signs of weakness, over eagerness to agree. If you appear too arrogant or aggressive there is a danger of alienating the negotiator or their advisor.

The element of surprise can be useful, particularly where the other negotiators are overplaying the status card. Inland Revenue investigators expect Businessmen to be on the defensive. Usually there is something to hide and the cards all seem to be stacked in the favour of the investigators who have strong powers and adopt a very threatening posture. Accountants will usually be compliant because a lot of their work will depend on their relationship with the Inland Revenue so they will tend not to be too assertive.

This is not really fair representation for the businessman. One businessman had quite an innovative approach to these negotiations. He brought in a top QC to the meeting, who was not even a tax barrister.

What he did was turn the table, i.e. started asking the investigators questions and forced them to adopt a different approach. I am not criticising the Inland Revenue but showing it as an example of how parties will often act a certain way if they have status control. The ironic thing is that good negotiators are like poker players and you never guess that on paper they are at a severe disadvantage on negotiations.

Attention to detail

Like much of business the deal is in the details. That is why using the 'what if' questions can be useful. If there is not enough clarification a minor point can be crucial later on. In an ideal world the deal should be run through a piece of software that could pick up the potential for miscommunication and conflict.

Opening Offers

Your opening offer is crucial. If you are too near to what you really want you will end up nowhere near it as in many cases the offer will be seen as an opening gambit and the other party will hope to get a much better deal. It may be better to make a tough opening offer provided it is still credible. You need to convince the seller that you still want to genuinely buy their product. It is also a good idea if you can convince the seller you do not have the funds to meet their opening offer.

You do need to be tough and refuse to be intimidated. You should never be giving one way concessions without getting something back. What you are trying to get across is a psychological message. If you want something it is going to cost you.

Posture Part 2

I do sympathise well maybe only for a moment with possible bargaining positions you find yourself in. If you are applying for your first job after University, you desperately want to get into publishing and this is the only offer you have received; or you have started a small business organising events. You have got no business in your first three months and now a local council has asked you to organise their Halloween firework display. Your natural response is 'where do I bite their hand off'?

However the negotiating part has two agendas. They don't want to overpay. However they expect any candidate worth their salt to negotiate. If they don't they worry whether they will be able to carry out the project the way it should be. Get the deal on the wrong terms you will find it hard to increase your salary or your price for future council projects. Yes there may be some deals or opportunities lost but much greater potential that when you get deals, you will get the right one. You cannot do every deal. I am reminded of an old John West Salmon advertisement "It is the fish that John West reject that makes John West the best". Some of the best deal making you do will be the deals you walk away from.

For instance everyone is into buy to let property and as a result there have been significant house rises and a great difficulty at the moment within the UK in getting rental returns to pay mortgage interest and expenses. So if you are a good business person you have got to search through a lot of bad deals to find the ones that are self funding. If you can make property deals that self fund you can do more. If you are having to pay part of the mortgage yourself and want to do more similar deals hoping for long term appreciation, your cash flow is potentially catastrophic. Your deal making skills come into play and you should never give anyone more power or leverage. Something it is natural to always assume the other party has something up their sleeve or hold all the cards. Sometimes it may be true, but often most of it is in their mind.

Remember Price is not the only Issue

As well as price in any deal you will have a number of related items products/services peripherals; the terms related to which could also be negotiated in the deal.

Keep your options open

It is always good to have other options, other than feeling under threat. If you are trying to up the price your major customer pays, you need to have sought out alternatives and if necessary be prepared to walk away if they refuse to budge. I always find it amazing how attractive an employee can become to an employer, when other people are offering them better packages to go and work for them. Again perception is important, and like much of your achievement a lot will depend not on the actual reality but how you value yourself because that is likely to be how others will value you as well. In an ideal world people will give you as much as you deserve, but that is not how it works in practice. If you want anything you have to ask for it.

I think we should end this section by looking at a short case study relating to negotiation and assertion to illustrate it is one of the core competencies you must develop. You may not be a capitalist but if you want to make things happen you will need to work with other people gather resources and implement. All stages require negotiation skills. Are you working on yours?

Case Study

Jean has been taken on as a graduate trainee by a local charity for the disabled. They want her to run a new project to raise £250,000 a year for the charity and to build up the volunteer base and corporate sponsorship for the charity. What situations and issues will Jean face where she may need her negotiation skills? (please spend 10 minutes on your answer before reading the next section).

Some Thoughts

Jean has got to be enterprising to set up a new innovative project and make it happen. Will she have to negotiate anything? Almost everything

- First of all she needs to agree the terms of your contract.
- Is it fixed term or permanent?
- What is her salary and benefit package?
- Jean needs to agree with her boss exactly what outcomes have to be achieved and within what timescale
- Jean needs to establish what resources are available.
- Does she have a marketing budget?

- Does she have the help of any paid or volunteer staff?
- Jean has to negotiate some type of reward systems if she makes the project successful
- Jean has to do deals with local companies and give them some key benefit
- Jean will design some type of deal for volunteers and look for negotiable benefits which might attract volunteers.
- Jean will need to do deals with stakeholders in all stages of the projects
- Jean should identify alternative sources of funding and negotiate a package which may fund the operation pending corporate or fund raising events
- Jean will look at what deals could bring in the £250,000 and negotiate terms and conditions
- Jean will need to negotiate with friends and family to get their support in her new job.

Conclusion

Hopefully you can see just because an area of work is not obviously a business venture, this does not preclude the need for negotiation. Some people seem to be born dealmakers. When I was nine I used to buy a quarter of sweets, take them to church and in the children's church sell sweets for the children's collection. This happened for three weeks until the helper put a stop to it. I was doing deals but actually as I focused more and more on my schoolwork, I didn't really build my dealing skills. As someone who just wants the job done , it is easy to do poor deals just to move a project on. However like many other people I have had to realise that almost anything in life is dependent upon a deal. If the deal is right everything will flow. Make a bad deal in business or personal life, and despite your best efforts, things will not work.

Observation

As well as practising some of the ideas contained here, I recommend you start observing people, during a dealing/bartering situation. If you find something useful try to apply it straight away.

Keep a mini record of your attempts at negotiating. Review every deal you make, no matter how small. What can you learn from this? You can also do deals on behalf of others. The ironic thing is because you are a third party and not emotionally involved you will do better deals for them than you do for yourself.

Never accept anything if people have favours or requests to make of you, what do you need from them?

At times we have been advocating a fairly hardnosed approach. However I am still not a fan of taking 100% and leaving the other party nothing. They are less likely to stick to the deal, and at the very best will tend to badmouth you. Try to be strategic; don't shoot yourself in the foot in the long run.

Try to be honourable but that does not mean saying yes to deals that don't suit you or are unfair. Every deal will be different; they will progress at different rates and will have their own subtle nuances. You need to apply the basic success principle. Know what you want before you start, do the negotiations, decide where to make the pitch and be flexible. Try to change what you can offer if there are particular needs and you are still getting what you want. Flexibility is the key and that includes getting out. Develop negotiation skills and I promise you, you will be welcome in any industry and will fare much better. In an ideal world the meek should prosper in our world business or personal, but always remember "blessed is the dealmaker"!

negotiating the deal

CHAPTER FOUR

PERSONAL BRANDING

PERSONAL BRANDING

Branding is not just a function needed by large or small organisations, it also requires an attitude of mind in your company or organisation which sets out to meet the needs of a defined market and organises all its activities to meet them. Likewise you also need to think of yourself as a company; a personal services company.

Whether you are setting up a business or working for a company, you are a one woman/man personal services company and you need to use the concepts of branding to get yourself the best deal in the marketplace.

Marketing the Brand

First it is necessary to carry out market research and then developing your own marketing mix to achieve your goals. There is an interesting book in America where a marketing consultant applies marketing concepts to the mission of finding a suitable husband or wife. This is not my area but its success as a bestseller illustrates the recognition that marketing techniques can be used in your career or business. It may also illustrate how desperate some people are to find a partner which may also provide a business opportunity for others!

You are the Brand?

Everyone knows about the Beckham brand. David and Victoria are recognised as a worldwide brand because they have been clearly marketed as such. Everything you do, wear or say adds to the perception other people have of you. You need to provide a clear image/impression you want to give and making sure you don't get involved in activities which conflict with the market you are aiming to reach.

I came across a young lawyer who was aiming to build a practice in a local town, focused on clients who were more likely to become long term customers. The image he needed to project was that of someone business like, a safe pair of hands respected in the local community.

To his cost he got involved in a "get rich quick" scheme which involved getting other people signing up and buying stock. Clients who came into his office to get advice about their legal structure found themselves being harangued to join the scheme. The young lawyer as is often the case didn't make any money out of the get rich quick scheme. More importantly he was not seen as the safe pair of hands. It was a big blow to his long term prospects of gaining any kind of local market share.

TASK

What type of brand image do you want to project: who is your customer?

Let us say for instance you want to appeal to one of the major consultancies such as Accenture (large technological consultancy firm). You need to find out early on what type of person they are looking for and what evidence you need to provide to attract their attention. If you found for instance they wanted someone enterprising who could take responsibility for projects, you would look at your track record and you could consider becoming an intern for the student enterprise centre; looking for some student activities such as the Faculty formal where you could take responsibility for making it happen.

The difficulty with this strategy is you may end up trying to change your personality and engaging in activities just to get a job with a company you admire, ignoring your own natural skills and competencies. It can seem to go against the advice "be yourself" or play to your strengths. The point is, it is important to identify what you are interested in and also what you are good at then use marketing strategies to achieve what you want. You may be the greatest talent the publishing industry has been looking for, but if they don't become aware of you and you don't get yourself into a position to show that you can make a contribution, then your chances of success are pretty slim. Many of you will be brought up to keep out of the limelight and not to put yourself forward. However it is a very competitive world and you need to get a competitive advantage; therefore, developing skills to assist in marketing yourself are a necessity.

personal branding

Market Research

If you are building a business, not only do you need to assess market need at the start of the business you need to ensure that 'keeping an eye on the market' becomes part of an ongoing company process. Markets will change and you need to change the focus of your products or services to meet changing requirements. The same applies to corporate or community careers. What are the key qualities needed? What does the market need?

Not only do you need to demonstrate market awareness regardless of industry, you need to know what the employment and business market is looking for. For instance many businesses and companies want their new graduates to be enterprising and innovative. How can you demonstrate these qualities and your capacity to act that way in the job situation? Are there courses being run in innovation? What type of work experience could you undertake during the holidays to further develop these skills?

Market research information can be accessed formally and informally. Read market reports on the trends in your industry, find out what statistical data says about the size of the market for your product. Informal information can also be useful. Knowing what is a key driver for a chief buyer in a major company or what are the major preferences of the recruitment team. I found informal information to be very useful prior to an interview for my first job in accountancy with a major industrial company. This was my one opportunity to get into an excellent training scheme. Informal information gathering allowed me to discover the main recruiter was only interested in employing trainee accountants who were committed to completing their accountancy qualifications. It was very useful to know this - I was genuinely committed to doing this but knowing his key preference ensured I focused on demonstrating my personal commitment to this process as well as demonstrating during the interview to him my views as to the importance of accountancy students being able to complete their professional exams.

Whatever your business ambitions, you need to have access to information. Building networks will help to access this information in addition to the normal access route from published market research. You must not ignore what the market tells you remember this is the main principal of marketing which separates it from selling.

What are your customers or potential customers saying?
What needs/benefits do they have?
Will they still be looking for the same thing in the long term?
Do their needs/benefits match with the product/service you offer?
If not, what value can you add to your offering to make it more likely that you can do business with them?
If you can't you may need to re-examine the market and look for a different niche to pursue.

Market research information is only of use if you base your activities on it. Never assume because you are in business or have experience of an industry that you know all the answers, you need to ask the market, respect it and adjust your marketing plan accordingly. You also must keep abreast of developments and respond appropriately. As a small business if you do not respond to changes your business is more vulnerable than a large organisation. In addition, as a small company one of your competitive advantages is you can react quickly, so keeping close to market changes should be easier for you. Your marketing should be focused on making a sale or getting that next contract and you need to do this following a clear strategy.
If you are the product where are you on the product cycle?
Where will the market be in five years time?
Will you be strategically positioning yourself to take advantage of opportunities that may become available?

TASK

Thinking about your own business idea what market information do you think you will need? How can you access this information without any major financial or time implication?

SWOT analysis

This is a standard tool used by companies to analyse their own position within a particular market niche. The initials reflect four areas of a company's strengths, weaknesses, opportunities and threats. Still keeping on the theme that you are the product in personal marketing it is important to analyse yourself with regard to the market you are going to target, having already carried out your market research.

What are your strengths with regard to the opportunity on offer?
What are your weaknesses?
What are the key opportunities that you could develop?
What are the threats that challenge your business venture or career opportunity?

Let us say you have decided to set up a student enterprise networking club.
What do you have to offer that will help develop the project.
Do you have contacts which will help?
Have you any marketing background or access to finance?

What weaknesses do you have as a recent graduate?
Is there something missing?
Do you have the influence to make things happen?
Have you experience of running such an enterprise before?
Do you have the necessary management skills?

Is there a clear opportunity now?
Is the opportunity local or is it nationwide?
Is the opportunity a good profit model or should it be a social enterprise?

What threats are there?
Is there a similar organisation that people can join?
What specific risk, financial or otherwise does the project have?

TASK

Do a SWOT analysis of yourself in relation to your business or career objectives. What does your SWOT analysis tell you?

Unique Selling Proposition

What is your Unique Selling Proposition (USP)?
What do you offer that nobody else does?

What is your competitive advantage?
What separates you from any other competitors?

Product

What service product or information are you offering the market place?
What are you actually offering?
What exactly will you do?
What is your proposition in one sentence?

Price

How do you price yourself in the market?
What are you worth?
What market are you after?
Where are you positioning yourself?
The price is a key component. How have you worked out your price? Are you prepared to hold out for it? Are you a £50/day £500 or £2000/ day person?

Place

How are you going to operate?
Is this going to be within a company or as a business?
Where will you reach your client?
Will you make use of modern technology?
How international is your product or service?
What is your distribution system?
How will people access you either within the company or in the world?
Have you the capacity to reach out to the emerging markets in India and China?

Promotion

It is important to have a good marketing mix. Your product, price and place must be in line with market information need. Having identified who and where your customer is, you need to market yourself to fit this market. The key part of the marketing mix is to make the market aware that you are available and have the appropriate skills and competencies to satisfy the market need. In some cases this may lead directly to a sale, however in many cases you and other key advisers may need to use personal influence based on an effective promotional activity to close the deal.

We are all a little bit uneasy as to how celebrities continually promote themselves or the lengths that those who fall off the ladder will go to get back in there. However if you want to make your business succeed; get that job; continue to access exciting opportunities you need to ensure you are comfortable with the concept of self promotion. It would be nice if your service or product was enough to ensure you got the results you required, but even in traditional professions everyone is aware of the need to make other people aware of who you are and what you do to increase your own brand.

Guerrilla Marketing

It would be nice to have a huge marketing budget unfortunately most of us do not therefore you will have to adopt the same strategy as many other small business owners. You will have to become an effective "Guerrilla Marketer", that is, you need to adopt promotional strategies which produce maximum results for the minimum expense. The key is maximum publicity and awareness as cheaply as possible.

PR

Many people do believe what they read in newspapers and magazine articles and many people still read both. Newspapers and magazines are always looking for interesting material or products which are likely to catch the reader's eye.

You need to look for opportunities to make the news. It is all about building a relationship either directly or indirectly with e.g. a PR consultant.

Networking

You need to harness the power of positive word of mouth. Join networks which help you meet people who are the important players in your field. You need to have a system to make contacts and also to keep in touch with them. No point in giving you business card to someone if you don't follow it up. A network almost has a financial worth. Some people in your network will know people, who know people who will be able to explain or help with key areas which could prove of use to your business or career. Again, it may not cost money directly but you may have to provide help to someone who you hope can assist you later. This kind of networking requires effort, planning and organisation. If you go to a networking event you should have set yourself goals for that event. On return review your performance and how effective you were on the day and then have a systematic way of keeping in touch with new contacts.

The key thing in personal marketing is that you want to use the power of word of mouth marketing. Networks are only one of a number of methods which could prove effective in getting the progression available from word of mouth marketing. What networks should you be joining to help you reach your target market?

Think about workshops or seminars you could attend; join relevant internet activities and any other form of interaction which may assist you in delivering effective word of mouth marketing.

The key lesson is you can't sit and wait for positive word or mouth marketing to work. You must positively influence the process and make sure that the most powerful tools are used.

Market Segment

Which market segment are you after? You can divide your potential customer group up accordingly to various factors including income, gender and region. You need to decide which segments you are after and why. For example if you target all small businesses with less than 5 employees you must be sure that this segment matches your strategic objectives. This group for example are unlikely to have a budget to fund growth consulting or training.

personal branding

TASK

Let us presume you decide you want to be a sales consultant for a pet products business. Divide up the possible market segments; decide which one to go after and why, don't try and target the entire market.

Market segmentation is important because your message needs to be understood clearly by one or two groups. You are likely to be less focused if your market is "everyone". Ideally as a business person it is good to find a niche where your experience and resources will leverage high results. Some use the phrase 'be an expert' in your field.

Packaging

How are you packaging yourself and your work? This can include dress and personal appearance. It can also include how services are laid out, how professional (or extensive) your portfolio appears.

Market Research

As mentioned earlier clever ongoing use of market information should lead to strategic shifts of marketing mix activities where this proves necessary.

Product Enhancement

You should be continuously trying to improve your knowledge, qualifications, and experience to enhance the "product" which in this case is you.

Branding

It is important you develop a brand which people recognise, to try to encourage customer loyalty. As part of the brand image you will have to consider the packaging appeal.

Product life cycle

For your business or your career you should analyse where it is in the product life cycle. For instance, if you decide to open a sandwich bar you need to remember this is not a new concept unless you have some very innovative features. You may decide you want to become a celebrity through the power of "reality TV". This particular market is extremely saturated hence your idea would need to be 'new and exciting'. Ironically a few of the business programmes are still at an early stage of their lifecycle and may provide a better vehicle for exploitation. You will need to come up with new strategies or markets for products reaching saturation point and you will also need a very effective guerrilla marketing system if you are at an early stage and looking to be a pioneer. There is a lot of hard work to do before proof of concept. Let us say you want to be England's first professional bullfighter; this idea would be at an early stage and you would have to adopt your marketing ideas appropriately.

Price

Your price will be affected by demand, to put it bluntly. You want to be a trainee lawyer. There are loads of law graduates looking for the places, so the legal firms can keep salaries down. The key question when looking at your business product is where do you see the pricing going in the long run and what is your strategy to get there?

Advertising

Advertising needs to be targeted with clear product measurable results. To create brand awareness you will get much greater impact by using more subtle methods, for instance you could offer to write a short piece in a newspaper column which could promote you as an expert. Selling your services following this more subtle route to advertising is more likely to be effective.

Ideally any form of promotion should be considered which could produce results. Particularly with professions there is a perception that any professional who has to advertise for work must not be very good. That is fine and dandy but how do you get work when you put that nameplate up and don't have a list of NHS customers? You need to promote not only to get business, but also to attract the type of work you are looking for in the long run.

For example, your long term strategy may be to work for an investment bank; presuming this is not immediately possible you may have to in the short term take a job in financial services. Where possible you can now promote yourself to a market segment that will have some type of link however tenuous with Investment banking. Interestingly enough many people have difficulty thinking strategically.

Whatever media you use you need to be clear what it is you want to achieve. One graduate started out as an architect and had a simple strategy 'to get as much work as possible'. He promoted himself everywhere and whilst this was effective in getting lots of small jobs he ended up with a reputation as "the cheapest in town". Two years later he found himself with lots of small work at a low margin and with not even the time to think of the large building contractor market he had originally hope to target. In the end he sold the practice and completely rebranded himself.

It is also hopefully obvious that you need to use a media which will reach your target audience. It may please friends and family to see your article in your local paper on your stock brokering expertise in London. Much more effective would be something read by people in the profession who may be looking to invest significant sums with a stock broker in your area.

AIDA

This should always be the underlying design model for any promotional activity you undertake.

A	Attention - make the customer aware
I	Interest - attract their interest
D	Deal - get them to deal with you
A	Action - get them to take some action steps

> ### TASK
>
> You are a newly qualified chartered surveyor and want to promote your career in commercial property in London.
> What 3 things can you do to make it happen?

Other promotional Activities

You can use free samples, point of sale displays, competitions or other numerous promotional techniques. Again it has to be suitable for you. Are you building a database? How can you get people to use the product or service even once?

For those of you who have a service, you don't quite have to go to the extent of the actor Claude Van Damme who did high kicks outside a restaurant where a Hollywood producer always dined.

However you get the idea. Find a way for a large company or customer to sample your services without any obligation.

The type of promotion does depend on:-

the stage the product is in its life cycle
the nature of the product itself
the amount of your budget
the nature of the target market
do you need to promote locally or internationally?

Public Relations

As well as using the media you can also give services or products "pro bono" and create awareness. It is vital you are also committed to the charitable organisation you are engaging with otherwise it could very easily turn to a negative public relations exercise. Celebrities have learnt to their cost that agreeing to work with a charity for profile and then maybe cancelling engagements in favour of more commercial opportunities has lead to negative publicity.

personal branding

Remember, you are a brand; you may not be under media scrutiny like the Beckhams but everything you do counts. If you are promoting an image as someone who supports family values, living the life of a playboy tends to place you in the position of being a hypocrite. The person who is clever at personal marketing will always be able to exploit most situations to their advantage.

Watch how other people market themselves?

Watch someone who is building a professional reputation or someone who is building a celebrity profile. What steps do they take? Observe the number of times they appear in the press covering a wide range of activities. We do love to see the celebs struggle, particularly the 'D' list, who have slipped from the 'B' list, and will do literally anything on TV to get their profile back. We enjoy it, particularly if it doesn't work.

However you can learn lessons. Celebs will spend at least 25% of their time promoting their profile. You need to invest at least 10% of your time no matter how busy you are in presenting yourself to the market and keeping your profile up. If you have one major customer or employer who is paying you very well it is natural to think why bother? However if you fall out with that key provider of income, suddenly you are in difficulty without the income or career profile to help your marketing activities. That is why there is the old truism from careers advisers, "It is easier to get a job when you have one".

I have observed some students who attend business events in their holidays to make contacts, have fun, and search for future opportunities. I see lots of others who can't be bothered and are "too busy" to explore these opportunities. Obviously I presume you are the active type if you have taken the time and effort to read this book.

Cross Fertilisation

You can be enterprising if you apply business practices which work in one industry to another. For instance, if you have worked in the highly competitive world of financial services where marketing is a key element you could use these strategies effectively in other areas. Maybe you end up working for a firm of architects perhaps adapting one of the marketing strategies from financial services could be highly innovative and profitable for the architectural practice.

The benefit of varied approaches

Depending on one client or one personal marketing strategy is not enough. I observed one young accountant who built his practice on designing and delivering start-up seminars for small business owners via the local enterprise agencies. Initially he got lots of business; however there were two problems with this, firstly although he got lots of business, he was not accessing established business owners (hence he lost valuable clients he had worked with) and secondly when the enterprise agencies cut costs by delivering these sessions themselves he had no alternative strategy. Different activities can help each other provided they are part of a co-ordinated plan. They open up your services to a wider variety of sources and each method of marketing will impact the other.

Your personal brand

Remember you are a brand and everything you do or say counts. This includes not only your activities but everything from your posture, voice, tonality and small talk. You may get a shock if you had to watch a video of your own technique when selling or networking. We would all prefer not to watch these films, but as you can imagine if you can relax you will learn a lot. This type of activity is used extensively for those who wish to work in areas such as counselling and can be extremely effective in getting rid of 'bad habits' – it gives us an opportunity to 'see ourselves as others see us'.

Online

Something you have to accept is that although "dot coms" are not necessarily always the favourite mode of business you must make sure your online profile matches up with the brand – that marketing message you want to present.

I learnt the following lesson in an interesting way. My ten year old son bored at school decided to "Google" his father. Sounds like a painful process but as the modern techno kid he is, he likes to use all available resources and gadgetry.

When I was "Googled" that is, looked up, he did find me at my place of work but found a very non-existent profile. Whose fault was this? None other than my own.

Nowadays the first thing people do if they are considering doing business with you or an associated company, is to use the power of internet to check you out.

Marketing practitioners reckon that as part of your personal marketing agenda you should be very careful with your marketing information. On the internet everything you do from your membership of online communities and active participation in them, should all fit clearly with your strategic marketing plan. As already highlighted earlier, word of mouth is very important and incorporating this via internet activity provides the opportunity to reach out worldwide. Branding is very much about the image that people have of you. It is sensible not to ultimately get too worried and expect everyone to like you. However, if you want to achieve significant career or commercial success you need to control to some degree the public's perception of you. The key question to ask your self is, 'do the right people notice what I do'? If no, you need to take corrective action. If your work is good you may think you will automatically achieve results, but sadly that is not how it always works, it is equally important other people hear what you can do.

As part of your personal branding try and focus more often on the type of activities which are more likely to get results. Is there a forum where you can provide information which lets other people know what you are doing e.g. a company newsletter. Company newsletters are always searching for newsworthy items. Remember you will always be communicating something about yourself, make sure it is the message you want to convey.

Opportunity

To stand out you or your company need to be different. You need to see things differently, that is why creativity and seeing different angles can be important. Being enterprising is all about open mindedness and being prepared to take action to do something. Again as suggested in the creativity session sometimes the new solution will come from looking at an industry or area that you have never considered before.

Using a range of activities is more likely to create opportunities.

Where are you now?

As you know I recommend you do try to measure where you are now. It is like the example I gave where I noticed that I was not paying enough attention to my online profile. Do something about it. It could be a shock for you to realise that your profile is not out there. Can you in one or two sentences explain exactly what you do for your employer or customer, what benefit you provide and what is your unique selling proposition. You then need to get that message out to the market via whichever 'guerrilla marketing' strategy you have chosen; being flexible along the way without losing sight of the end objective. Running about at breakneck speed will not necessarily achieve anything if you have been strategic in your planning, ensuring all you effort is geared to the right audience, at the right time with the right message, you should achieve results.

Relationship marketing

People are very wary of those who suddenly become their best friend to achieve a marketing objective and then disappear until they need something again. A lot of your long term marketing benefit will come from people you deal with time and again who trust you.

Who are you focusing on?

I am trying to get you to work on your self promotion; however I must also urge you to do this with the focus on others. Are you constantly trying to give your audience/clients what they want? You may need to demonstrate this clearly and often to your audience. Ensuring the marketing philosophy is part of your belief system will pay dividends.

It is obvious if you have your own business you need to do this, however even in the world of work within an organisation it is important to think about how other people perceive you. Why are they dealing with you? What result are they looking for? And what impact can your activities have? Could you do anything more to make a greater contribution?

If you want to do work for a new customer, find an opportunity to do something on a small scale to demonstrate your worth.

Always Deliver

Whatever marketing activity you can undertake, whoever you are marketing to, one of the key messages is you must always deliver what you promise. This will shock people as it turns the normal strategy of "over promise/under deliver" on its head.

Learn from companies

Look at how major brands achieve success – What is it about NIKE or McDonalds etc that make you want to use them, rather than the opposition? How can you use this in your own case? What strategies worked for them and how might these work in a variety of different settings?

Testing

You may not be a business but it is always important to test what is working. Where is the profile coming from? What are you getting out of it? You need to track responses but also the difference between people who have noticed, and those who have as a result of your marketing actively engaged with you.

The whole concept of personal marketing is not just to get some recognition of you as a brand but also some tangible results. Following Paretos Law (a favourite of mine I know) 20% of your activities will yield 80% of the results, therefore you need to identify which activities are the most effective.

Explore different events which may yield results. Engaging in personal presentations,

Sending out e-mails, attendance at events, online profile – which is working most effectively? Can you change your approach a little in each and measure the result? Small changes can be the levering point to lead to overall significant improvement.

Endorsement

The endorsement of key influencers will always play a significant part. Always try and include personal endorsements of your work.

> ### TASK
>
> How do you market yourself? Break down the process. Set up a system to measure the performance of each part of the process.

Relationships

Systematically building relationships with other people and organisations where you will actively seek information and help each other is very useful. Always try to assist other people you want to work even before a deal is struck. You need to formally look for referrals or chances to do interesting projects. Always be willing to help anyone within your organisation with new projects.

If you own a business you are attempting to find the ideal customer who needs the benefits that your products or services can bring. The clarity in knowing the end customer, their needs and what particular problems they have are vital before system design. The same applies internally within organisations or communities. Who could be a key influencer in your career and what could you contribute to help them with their performance.

When someone is running a business most people can accept the need for a formalised referral process. Some describe this as a manip-ulative process and often in the corporate world it is referred to as "office politics". I have often sympathised with this viewpoint how-ever we are talking about you achieving your goals and in reality this is not always an easy process. If you leave things to chance there is little chance of you making an impact. If you refuse to personally market yourself you fail to make others aware of what you can do and ultimately the opportunity to work with them. It is up to you.

Clients or contacts you have lost

You will find out the hard way in business. You will have disagree-ments with people both internally and externally no matter how honourable your intentions. The key is to part as amicably as possible and to make an effort to keep in touch to lessen the possible impact of any disagreements for the long term. You, your position, and circumstances may have changed so it could be useful to get in touch again and try to rebuild the relationship. If you have not already dealt with the cause of the disagreement, now is the time to do so. People who are generally successful in business do make considerable efforts to rebuild relationships.

Other Promotional Tools

How do you keep people informed with regard to your current activities?

Direct mail and/or email using a structured format can keep you in touch with your client base.

Use the Internet

Use the internet to target any possible key prospects.

Go through your contacts

Sit down and go through your contacts, internal and external. Divide them into appropriate categories. You need to identify people who either individually may need your services or may have connections with others who may be interested in the services you office. You are searching for trends or connections to ensure your system is as efficient as possible. Whilst you may not have the resources to undertake personal marketing at the celebrity level you should still use the Paretos law and get 80% of your results from the 20% of your time invested. Think about these contacts or target group and vary the strategy you to approach them. It may well be a short email or written note followed up by a phone call. Care does need to be taken when using emails as often messages can be interpreted as either too friendly or abrupt.

It is often much more effective to try and make personal contact so make sure you keep attending as many events which are likely to raise your personal profile.

Your own website

Creating a website is cheap and relatively easy however maintaining it requires a greater commitment from you. Deciding what you want the website to be able to do is a good starting point; is it just information or do you need a much more interactive site. Remember this is part of your marketing strategy. The creation of a virtual community with similar interests to you may be one option which increases your profile, and also increases your access to knowledge and possible collaborators for projects.

A small company I know has 24 different websites aimed at 24 different niches.

The other key potential is that you can reach out on a global basis without necessary leaving your office. Potential business may come from the new emerging economies as well from local/national markets.

Creative Marketing budget

If your budget is small you could perhaps work with a marketing contact offering some of your products/services in return for marketing help.

TASK

Make a list of all the products/services your company offers. Make a list of the people you deal with. Make a list of external stakeholders. Can you see any connections between the lists? Are there any communication lines that need to be established? List any other stakeholders you would like to add to the list.

Keeping in contact

You can see there are so many things to do. How do you maintain contact with all these people? You need to keep communication lines open with people who are important to you. The type of communication is also important. Some of you will be calling this chapter "the how great thou art" chapter as I seem to be advising you to "blow your own trumpet". I am certainly advising you to make others aware of your achievements using communication via your contact list with a particular focus on their link to your service/product. Remember make the list, use the list and don't lose contact with people.

A Marketing Plan

You need a plan with a set of goals and measurable events eventually leading to the end product. Again it is what you do on a weekly basis rather than once a year which will determine whether your marketing strategies are a success. It is too easy when things are going well with one project, to forget to take time out to work on your marketing strategy. However the plan forms the basis of your work, the feedback you receive and future marketing strategies you may have to use. Whether you work for a company or run your own company marketing is a key life skill. It will decide ultimately how successful your career or business is. Devote at least 3 hours per week to marketing, much more if you are in business. It may not seem important. I remember as a businessman trying to set aside one afternoon a week for marketing. This was a strategic move and I ought to be congratulated. However I didn't do it as I found I was able to generate (initially) so much work and as "time is money" and I wanted to invoice as much as possible, I just overwhelmed myself with work. Unfortunately I came to regret ignoring the marketing side of my business as I realised that others had positioned themselves to accept only certain types (usually higher rate of return) of work. Sometimes people are initially lucky and by good luck find themselves in a lucrative market however they may run into problems when there is a need to change.

Above all realise you do have a lot to offer. How can you do more? How can you reach more people or make an impact? Use marketing effectively.

TASK

Make one final plan on one A4 page only. Who is your market? What services/product do they need? How will you reach them? How will you use marketing on an ongoing basis to maintain and grow your relationship with them.

Marketing is for life!

personal branding

CHAPTER FIVE

FEAR OF FINANCE

FINANCE

"Show Me The Money"

Money makes the world go around and I want to convince you to take it seriously. People generally fall into two camps, those who are obsessed by money or those who completely disregard it. Our 'attitude to money' is something which is generally not discussed in schools and little education is given on how to manage it. At University only students who study finance or accounting are provided with an understanding of the topic. Generally speaking the rest of the student population are left bamboozled with a mix of complex formulae and jargon which sends them off to sleep. I have experienced Chief Executives who cringe when they have to look at a financial report; I have also met with Accountants and Bank Managers who have no idea how to build wealth.

Whatever your motivation for pursing a job, idea or project do not underestimate the importance and value of understanding money. I do not want to turn you into a modern day scrooge who despite vast wealth makes no contribution to others and lives a miserable existence. Ebenezer still exists you know. I met one multi millionaire five years ago who was being sued by a 65 year old who had worked for him for twenty years as a van driver being paid £1-20 per hour. When I asked the old gent why he was bringing the case he explained. Last year after nineteen years of employment his boss had told him he was buying him Christmas dinner for the first time. Touched by this kind gesture he noticed the following day something has been posted through his letter box at his house. When he opened the door there was a chicken leg wrapped up in tin foil. His Christmas dinner! Needless to say he wasn't impressed and sued.

However money can also play a significant role even if you are involved in an organisation whose motivation is not solely about profit. Community organisations spend their time starved of resources and public sector organisations now have to be accountable financially, this now also includes Universities.

Many people have a phobia about money, accounts and anything to do with numbers. Usually it starts with difficulty with Maths at School and the creation of a fundamental belief "I hate numbers, I'm useless at Maths and will never be able to handle money"!

I do understand the frustration people experience as a lot of time at school is spent doing the kind of maths e.g. algebra, geometry and various other areas which go beyond the ability to add up with a calculator. For the purposes of the E Factor all you have to learn is how to use your calculator to do maybe some multiplication at most. Follow my 'maths path' and I promise you will have a greater understanding of money and its importance in terms of your effectiveness regardless of which area you currently work in; private, public or community . What is important is not only that you understand the part money plays in business/community ventures, but also what your financial aims are.

The Realities of Money

The reality is you will spend a substantial part of your life working to either make or earn money to fund your life, the life of your loved ones and also to provide enough money to fund your retirement.

For some of you at University level you may feel that money does not matter and that community or social issues and doing what you enjoy is all that is important. However many of today's students are also living in a financial climate where student loans and part time jobs are the norm. Also your parents may be trying to encourage you to finish off your training as a chartered surveyor when all you want to do is to travel before joining the world of work. The last thing I want to do is to "rain on your parade" and yes, travel and freedom are great at any stage. What I would like to do is assist you to make decisions with an understanding of money and what the future may hold financially.

Do I Want Wealth?

I do understand that your priorities may change, but it is important to think where you are now and where you would like to end up financially. That interesting post in the civil service may appear attractive now after years of student penny pinching, but there is one thing for sure, you will never be wealthy. Public sector jobs do offer index-linked pensions and challenging work, however these are not a path to financial independence. People do change and the person who is happy today to get a public sector job now may well evolve into someone else, who in ten or fifteen years time realises they want a

fear of finance

different financial reality. Maybe you can leave and set up your own business but the odds are against you with years of pubic sector working and a secure job, and the commitments you will probably have gathered up.

Please do not misunderstand me; I am trying to ensure that you make a strategic decision about the financial rewards likely when you go into the world of work. Entering the public sector is unlikely to provide you with great wealth and you need to do this with your eyes open.

If wealth is something you would like to have, private enterprise is the best chance. Certain professions are also more likely than others to provide significant income opportunities, although most are more likely to lead to financial comfort rather than wealth and total financial freedom.

Dentists, Doctors, Lawyers and Accountants are amongst those who should do comfortably. One local businesswoman I know who has six daughters, all went into investment banking; a very lucrative sector as far as the world of employment goes.

Parental values may also have some effect on the decisions you make and I do understand the worries and concerns as a parent. You want your child to have an enjoyable and worthwhile career as you have had yourself (or not as the case may be). You don't want your child to face the uncertainty of self employment and entrepreneurship. You notice that the local dentist or lawyer tend to live in the bigger houses, drive the BMW's and have a good lifestyle. You then subtly encourage little Johnnie to go down that path. Forgive us parents as often our intentions are good but based on little information a lot of the time.

Do What You Love

If you genuinely like something you will show lots of interest and take extra care in your work. Normally this will lead to excellent performance.

I do subscribe to a certain extent to the dictate "do, what you love and the money will follow". If you choose psychology as your area to specialise in this is not recognised as highly in the "parental profes-sional" status file. However if you are a very good psychologist with some of the E Factor skills outlined here, particularly personal mar-keting, you can do very well. However, this is where an understand-ing of business/finance matters as this may assist you in taking the correct (more profitable road). Many of the psychology jobs avail-able are in the public sector and whilst these will result in a fairly comfortable life style this may not be for everyone. If you choose to take a more enterprising approach to your career development the route may result in higher rewards financially. Please don't think I am demeaning the path towards working in any particular sector, I just want you to make career and business decisions based on your long term financial values and goals. So firstly do what is it you enjoy (e.g. Psychology), but make sure you take a path which may provide a more lucrative financial return. Additionally you can often explore early on (if you are enterprising) which options in your cho-sen field open up possibilities for greater finanical return at a later date.

The same applies to working in the private sector. If you are a mechanical engineer and you spend the first ten years of your career in the cigarette manufacturing industry you may well become an expert in cigarette machinery. This may not always be transferable to other industries and you may have committed your career to what is essentially a declining industry due to worldwide trends.

Employment or Self Employment

I want you to be as enterprising as possible; therefore I should be rec-ommending you all to the world of self employment. However, there are advantages and disadvantages and you need to think carefully about these before joining the world of the self-employed. Employment with a large multinational can offer a number of bene-fits which self employment or employment with a community office cannot.

You know exactly where you are financially and can therefore plan more easily for savings, mortgages etc. However, you will pay PAYE which means Tax and National Insurance will be deducted from your gross pay at source with very little room for expenses or allowances. This means that as regards net income you will possibly be less well off than someone earning the same gross fees through self employment. What I do advise you to do whether as a self employed or employed person, see yourself as a "provider of services" and make sure you are getting the best possible return both financially and in terms of career prospects and professional development.

Having attended a recent Scottish Institute of Enterprise conference I was pleased to see that a number of major corporate employers are actually looking for employees with the Enterprise Skills that form part of the E-Factor.

In making your career decision at this stage, look at where the long term career path will lead in terms of personal development and financial reward.

It may be difficult for you to assess at this stage. A managing director earning £150,000 for a major company can seem like a dream, when you have just finished your daily shift at McDonalds at £4.15 per hour. However remember it costs £750,000 to buy a reasonable house in London and as an employee your £180,000 is approximately £75,000 net, £6000 a month. Add a couple of kids and any other dependents at home, the 70hrs a week the job demands is not quite as attractive as it first appears.

However for the 'Enterprisers' remember if the company has a good training programme and offers significant early opportunities for training and responsibility it is a chance to learn some of your mistakes as part of your experience. I am all for "the school of hard knocks" but too many too early in your career could put you out of the running for a long time.

Self Employment

I am one of those people whose mission is to encourage other people (in particular graduates) to start their own business particularly Global Business. Whilst encouraging them I also need to ensure they understand the financial advantages and disadvantages of self employment. In the following section I will explain both and then give you a strategy to boost the finances of both the employed and self-employed whatever route you choose.

Financial Advantages of Self Employment

One of the biggest advantages is the tax implications. A self employed person is able to claim a much greater range of expenses against their taxable income. Let us compare the case of an 'employed' and 'self-employed' chartered surveyor earning gross income of £50,000. The employee will pay approximately 50% of their income as tax and national insurance whilst the self employed person will pay virtually no national insurance saving almost £5000. In addition the self-employed person is able to claim (as deductible from income) all sorts of expenses. The running costs of the car used, travel, and wife's wages if she helps with the business, going to exhibitions, indeed anything which could be related to pursuing the business. This could perhaps knock off say, in net tax terms up to another £5000. Quite significant! Now it's not always this straightforward but there is a significant tax advantage.

There is also no cap on how much income you can charge for your services. You charge what you are worth. You are only limited by the time you can spend and what your client will pay. There is no limit to this if your business is providing information or products. You can also hopefully make money (indirectly) from people who work for you.

Disadvantages

These are the key self employed financial disadvantages:-

Cash Flow

Your ability to pay your bills and reinvest can be determined by when your clients pay you. If you are lucky enough to run a cash business such as a coffee shop or a pub, it is accepted practice to pay for your coffee or your beer at the point of purchase. However if the standard procedure for your business is to invoice your customers, then to a certain extent you are at the mercy of the company who owes you money. Even more, if your customers are a large company and decide not to pay you for a couple of months, there is probably not a lot you can do despite government 'late payment' legislation. Meanwhile you may be relying on your bank manager to help you pay your creditors unless your creditors will give you a similar payment time period to the time offered by your customers.

fear of finance

Risk

The other key financial indicator is risk. You do risk financial failure in running your own enterprise. You will operate in an uncertain environment. Arguably though, this applies equally to large companies, even in traditionally safe sectors such as Banking or Teaching.

Conclusion

Whether you are ready to run your own enterprise is up to you. There is lots of support available, and to be honest you can cut down your personal risk with limited company status (see streetwise guide by Dave Marshall Ryan details in bibliography).

However some of the enterprise skills I am trying to teach you in this book will be learned more effectively from running your own business.

There are various half way house solutions. Start a part time enterprise as long as it is not against the regulations of your employer, create a tax loss and set it against your PAYE tax.

Sign up for any kind of experiential learning which aims to allow you to do things, and gain experience the rollercoaster of business in a safe environment. An example of this is the television reality show "The Apprentice" where the contestants get opportunities to put into practice the skills we are talking about here. There is no doubt that there is nothing like the real thing. I am not saying you have to set up a large business and take all the risks, but any venture, even part time, will yield a lot of the lessons and make you "streetwise". What is important is that you treat community as well as business ventures as financial challenges and learn the financial reality through your experiences. Also be clever enough to learn from both successful and unsuccessful business people. If I was going to give you another enterprise skill it would be to continuously learn.

You will make mistakes, learn from failure, and don't make the same mistakes twice.

So let's continue with finance; if you can take on board some of these new ways of thinking and let them become part of your normal behaviour you will see positive changes in your world, be that business or the work place.

TASK

Have a go at setting out your financial goals. What would you like to be earning in a year, five years, ten years? What type of lifestyle would you like to lead?

Business Finance

Handling money in your own venture demands certain skills/ disciplines because of the uncertainty and risk of business. Get the fundamentals right and it will improve your chances of making your enterprises work. This approach can also be applied to corporate/ community ventures and indeed to your personal finances.

Cash is King

Cash flow rather than profit dictates the survival of a business. You can be making money on paper but if it is not there when you have to pay certain bills you are potentially insolvent at that moment.

Let me illustrate this. You are running your own business. Over the past three months. Your sales are £1,000 month 1, £2,000 month 2 and £3000 month 3, and you have to pay expenses of £1500 every month. Even though your sales are £6000 and expenses £4500, you are going to have cash flow problems, because you are paid two months in arrears.

The business will gradually catch up as your sales are more than expenses, but at the moment you can't pay your bills without the help of the bank.

That is why planning your financial budget is always important but particularly for businesses, so that you can cover the periods that cash flow will be slow. You have also got to be tough at credit control and insist on getting paid as quickly as possible.

fear of finance

Month 1	Month 2	Month 3
Cash in Nil	Overdraft at bank £1500	Overdraft at bank £3000
Cash out £1500	Cash in Nil	Cash in £1000
	Cash out £1500	Cash out £1500
You are now overdrawn at the bank by £1500	You're overdraft is now £3000	You're overdraft is now £3500

All businesses/organisations pay a lot of bills. If they think you are quite relaxed about getting paid, guess what, you go to the back of the queue!

Spell out your credit terms to your customers and adopt a fair but firm policy. Otherwise even when you are making money it will be in your creditors' bank accounts.

Profit

Although cash flow is vital to keep bills paid, it is important to realise that you are in business to make a profit, and even as a community or public sector organisation you do not want to have a deficit but want to at least break even.

Believe it or not you can get so busy doing the work and running an operation that you can lose track as to why you are in business.

TASK

Look at your financial budget for the next 6 months. Are you sure enough cash is coming in to enable you to meet outgoings. How can you plan for this?

Stuart Wilde an author on spiritual enlightenment launched a world-wide business a number of years ago. As you can imagine the people who ran his companies were more interested in their karma or spirituality than in the performance of the business. Like Stuart they wanted to save the world but he gradually realised that his business was not performing.

Stuart Wilde hit on a novel way of letting his managers understand the realities of business. After enduring phone calls for a month about how much they were enjoying their meditation sessions and how good they felt their karma was, Stuart used a different strategy to shake them up.

He would ring them every day once a day and ask "how many, how much" and then slam the phone down. After two weeks they got the message. Stuart wanted to know how many books they were selling each day, and how much their turnover was. The business changed and their attitude changed. They still wanted to save the world but they knew they had to make the business viable to do this. If you are in business, no matter what contribution you make, you are in it to make and collect the money. There is no other reason to be in business. Lose sight of this and your business will be in trouble.

Even in community or public sector organisations where you may not have the profit motive but you are judged on the efficiency of your operation, future funding and budgets depend on this. I still don't want you to make money your goal, but you have to operate within financial constraints and handle money or it will handle you!

Pricing Margin

Getting your pricing right and controlling your costs in line with this margin and volume, are key variables in whether a venture will work or not. Ideally you want as good a margin as you can get. You also need to ensure you are still getting the appropriate margin and/or return on your time. You should only sacrifice margin for a large enough volume of work.

fear of finance

Whether you are running your own business or working for a company, you should always measure the return you are getting for the effort put in. Remember self employed or employed, you are giving your skills for an adequate return. Every hour you spend working is an hour with an opportunity lost.

So get the appropriate price. As a business you need to remember that you have to recover both direct and indirect costs. Pricing also has psychological aspects. How much do you value yourself and your contribution/product?   There is no point in quoting a price of £1000 per day for your work for a community budget which has a maximum budget of £500 per day. However perhaps you should contribute in another way, or work in another market where there are financial rewards appropriate for your valuation of you own contribution.

Particularly with personal services, there is an element of what you charge is the worth you attribute to yourself. I am sad to disillusion you, but the old truism that if you don't value yourself, nobody else will. If you sell your services for a cup of coffee, then that is all the other party will offer.

The Bottom Line

"The bottom line is relentless"

Gaining some financial knowledge will help you make decisions. You must be sure that you are getting your profit margins, or in a community project that you are meeting the financial criteria set.

Income Should Exceed Expenditure Go!

You must always act according to your means. It is important to dress well and act the part of where you want to end up, though not if this involves taking on massive financial commitments for which you are not ready. For instance, as a trainee architect earning £10,000 per year, would you feel that you need to drive a 7 series BMW at £600 a month leasing cost?

Keeping Your Head

Assume your small business starts to perform well and you suddenly have money in the bank or have got a substantial salary increase. This is your defining moment. Can you do a Rudyard Kipling and "treat triumph and disaster just the same"? It goes without saying that keeping a cool head when you are in financial difficulty is important and obvious. Equally difficult though, is keeping a cool head when things seem to be taking off. With self employment in particular even if your own business is riding high at present, there is no guarantee that it will be the same in the next calendar year. You will also be liable to pay approximately 1/3 rd of your ill gotten gains to the tax-man at the end of the year, so put some aside, retain some for tax and by all means enjoy some of it.

Financial Documents

We have already talked about cash flow, profit and balance sheets. It is important that you understand what financial documents mean if you are either a 'would be' or an actual Entrepreneur. For enterprising corporate or community people, an understanding of these documents will advance your career. Arguably using the documents as a tool for personal, financial planning can help you achieve your financial goals.

Profit and Loss

Let us do a simple profit and loss statement for 1 year. Let's say you run a restaurant.

Sales	300,000
Cost of Sales	150,000
Gross Profit	150,000
Running Expenses	135,000
Net profit	15,000

The profit and loss measures your gross margin after the manufacture of your product, and the net margin after all claimed expenses.

Your <u>gross</u> margin is $\dfrac{150{,}000 \quad \text{gross profit}}{300{,}000 \quad \text{sales}}$

$= 50\%.$

Every time you spend 50p making and selling the product you make £1. This is average for the restaurant industry.

Your <u>net</u> margin is $\dfrac{£15000 \quad \text{net profit}}{£300{,}000 \quad \text{sales}}$

$= 5\%.$

Every time you have £1 of sales you are claiming 5p. This document includes all sales whether paid or not and all running costs whether paid or not. So you can make a profit on paper – but if the cash flow is not right you can still be struggling.

The gross margin above is really a test of operational efficiency. The net margin reflects whether the overheads or running costs are in line with the net profit. Again whether in business or personal life it is very easy for costs to exceed income and in particular to exceed cash flow.

Money spent unnecessarily is an opportunity missed for saving business and long term strategies. However I don't want you to turn out to be like a certain 70 year old multi millionaire I met recently, who was almost in tears as he told me he could now afford to go to Scotland thanks to Easyjet's low airfares. I don't think he was getting the full benefit of his money.

The Balance Sheet

The Balance sheet is another of those financial statements which you should know about whether as a business or individual. It is a snapshot of what you are worth at any one particular moment in time.

Examples

You are a forty year old male. You own your own house worth £200,000 and have £20,000 savings in the bank. You have a mortgage of £100,000.

Your Personal Balance Sheet as at today's date

Assets

House	£200,000
Savings	£ 20,000
Total Assets	£220,000

Liabilities

Mortgage	£100,000
Net Worth	£120,000

This man has items worth £220,000 but owes £100,000 against these. After paying all his bills, he is worth £120,000.

The key to long term financial success either as an individual or a business is to build a strong balance sheet. A pension is ultimately an asset, a sum of money from which eventually you can have an income, or buy an asset such as a business property, or any other investment in time or money.

Some people are lucky to be given gifts of shareholdings in lucrative family businesses or property portfolios. For the rest of us it is necessary to build a portfolio of assets. For those of you particularly in the public sector or working with a major corporate entity, your aim will possibly be focused on establishing a pension. Clearly there is nothing wrong with this, except that in many cases due to the changes in population etc. there are not many pension schemes which offer a guaranteed excellent return. You should therefore think about building some assets for yourself to lessen your risk and give you a better return.

The danger of having a high powered job at say £100,000 a year, or a small business making you the same, is that you are unlikely to build assets unless you deliberately set out to do so. As an employee your company will hopefully have some type of pension scheme, as self employed will have a better net income due to tax advantages. However in either case, if your lifestyle matches your income, and you don't create a surplus which can be used in an enterprising and innovative way, you are likely to struggle financially in the long term.

fear of finance

> **TASK**
>
> Draw up your own balance sheet now. Be honest. It is not where you are now that matters, but where you are going to end up. Check it at least once per year. The better the balance sheet, the greater the freedom you have to do what you want. To increase this freedom you have to act strategically, though this may be something which is very difficult when you are young, and which can look pointless when you are old.

Financial Strategy

Being strategic is being able to look beyond the next five years. To get where you want to be in the long term, live for the moment but the decisions you make now will have consequences in the long run. Unfortunately both businesses and individuals often seem to vary between the cost conscious scrooge type, and the party animal type who whatever he earns, he spends more. Some people get confused as to how pop stars and celebrities, or even business people who earn millions can end up with nothing. It is quite simple. They gross a million on which they owe say £400,000 tax. They party and spend the million, and the following year (as can happen in any business) they earn very little. The problem then is that they owe £400,000 tax, have no money to pay it, and no money to sustain their new lifestyle. Before you think that I am turning into a bore, I do appreciate a quote attributed to George Best a former Northern Ireland Footballer who spent his way through a few millions in his time, "I spent most of it on wine, women and parties. I wasted the rest", or the quote from the elderly porter in an Edinburgh hotel who delivered champagne to Best's hotel room when he was staying during the time Best played matches for Hibernian. Best had won £10,000 in the casino and was sitting with his girlfriend, ex Miss World Mary Stavin, and the porter said "Mr Best, where did it all go wrong"?

The answer is to have a strategy. If you have a business, try to reinvest a portion of the profits. The first person you should pay at least 10% is to yourself, before you start to spend your daily living costs"

Also set aside 10% which you spend now on whatever you want.

I don't want you to become an accountant. I wouldn't recommend it. I believe you should be taking calculated risks, and accountants like bank managers tend to be very good at analysing things, tearing them apart and rejecting them. They often count the beans for the success-ful enterpriser/ E Factor person. However you should take on board their good qualities. When you are spending money, it is good not to get too emotionally attached to material things, otherwise you will either buy them when you can't afford them, or pay too big a price for them. For example, let's say you see a flat that you want costing £100,000 when you have just started your first job. Your friend an estate agent says it is a good buy at £100,000 maximum price, but the bidding goes up to £130,000 and you still try to buy it. You are clearly "emotionally attached" to buying something at the wrong price.

Cash Flow Forecasting/Budgeting

Not another financial document. "I knew it, he is trying to turn us into an accountant after all" I hear you say!

The issue simply is that it is a good idea, particularly for a business, to plan ahead for income and expenditure and how the cash is likely to come in and go out of the business. The timing of cash flow can play a particularly important part. Sods law dictates that all your major bills will become due when income is unlikely to be available for banking. If need be, you should arrange overdraft facilities to ensure that you don't have a financial "melt down" situation. This budget is often known as a business plan. It enables you to plan ahead and make sure you can deal with financial uncertainty.

If you are not keeping within your budget, you need to take correc-tive action at an early stage to get back on track.

It is a bit late as a businessperson to realise that you are having money problems after the bank begins to return your cheques. This issue is critical for a business, and still important as an individual. There are some simple software systems available which can roll out budgets based on entering a few statistics. Use one to keep track and enjoy yourself without compromising your financial strategy.

fear of finance

Here is what a budget should look like. Don't be dazzled by the reams of figures. It is simply a list of your planned spending and income receipts over the period of Budget.

Jaynes Consultancy six month cash budget

	1	2	3	4	5	6
Income	0	0	0	2000	3000	2000
Expenditure						
Costs	1000	1000	1000	1000	1000	1000
Salary	1000	1000	1000	1000	1000	1000

TASK

Does Jayne have a cash flow or profit/ problem? Look at the figures. I will give you the answer on page 120

Conclusion

Money is only a resource to be used to enable you to develop a business and live your life to the fullest. Unfortunately many people are unable to handle money and it takes away from their enjoyment of life. I am simply trying to warn you that unless you go and live in a cave, it is very difficult to avoid money. Let us say you despise business you want to do good, and go and work for a charity for disabled people. As their manager what will be the first document you look at that will govern how you run the charity? Yes, the budget. You have to live within your funding to keep the community work going. For me it is simply a tool which if carefully used can enhance the contribution of your business, and help you do what you want with your life. I know it is difficult, particularly for those of you who may not need to think about it, and who have a simple solution to all financial issues in life. All I can say is handling money cleverly is part of the enterprising person's make up. They may look for specialist financial advice when required, but they usually consider the financial consequences of their decisions and make the right moves to get what they want. I respect those of you, who unlike me, refuse to contemplate becoming a millionaire. However money can play such a part in blocking business start up or growth. Many good people end up working forty hours a week just to live a fairly mundane life.

I feel if you have an enterprising/innovative capacity you deserve to have the opportunity to apply this, to live life and to help others. Don't let the lack of key financial strategies hold you back!

Raising Money

Any enterprise business or community has to raise money to start up, grow or survive.

My belief is that if the project is good enough, there is money available somewhere. Your job is to find it, and persuade the funders to back you. This applies even if you work within a large company where senior managers will have to agree to include your project within their budgets.

In raising funds, your personal influence and marketing skills will help in building your financial acumen and results. You will quickly realise that not every one will agree to back you. For instance let's say you are opening a new juice bar in your local town. You have just graduated and you ask your local bank manager to lend you £5000 but he refuses. For some people a rejection is a real blow, and you may simply give up the idea of starting your own business. The reality is that as a young person with no capital and no assets to secure a loan against, you are a bad risk. However if you research available information you will find there are specialist loan and grant schemes available to help people under 30 start their own business and a range of other options are also available.

What Will Funders Want to Know?

They will want to see your business plan, your budget and the reasons why you need the money. However it is not only the business model which is being evaluated, your ability to manage is also under review. Will you stick at it? Will you sell and make it happen? Accessing funds can be very much a selling exercise both on paper and in person.

ANSWER TO JAYNES CONSULTANCY PROBLEM.

Jayne has initial cash flow problems which will turn around in month 3.

Debt

There is good debt and bad debt. Loans, to buy a range of consumer goods are only to be recommended on a limited basis, for example, some type of mortgage to purchase property and a possible car loan are acceptable. Too much consumer debt can mean you have to work 40 hours a week simply to service your loans and pay your credit card debt.

Innovation Financing

Ideally you should always be looking for creativity in finding your funding for projects and personal ventures. It is obviously a good idea to find out whether any grants are available as this is free money that does not have to be repaid. There are lots of funds available, but you need to find out whether you can meet their criteria.

Private Investors

I am not recommending that you sell part of your family home to someone else, but in business ventures not enough enterprisers look for investment from outsiders. There are many external "Business Angels," who are successful business people who want to invest money in a venture with a possible long term return, or even in community ventures which meet their strategic charity obligations.

Leverage

I want to introduce you to the concept of 'leverage'. This consists of making money, or achieving results using other people's money, time or resources. It does sound like the original 'capitalist' concept i.e. 'get the factors of production, work them into shape whatever the consequences, and keep all the filthy lucre yourself.'

However that is not what leverage is about. It is time to have a few more reality checks.

Unless you are a pop star, a famous sportsperson or a very exceptional Chief Executive, there is a limit to what you can achieve in your own time. If you are going to set up a charity, unless you are already wealthy you are going to have to use someone else's money to fund your project and the time of volunteers to make it happen.

Ideally in today's environment I would always recommend that you try to use leverage wherever you can. You have only limited time, and you do not want to work all the hours available just to get by because you have a private life, family and friends who need some of your time, and you need to preserve a work/life balance to have the best possible chance to cope with stress and to keep healthy.

It can be a quality of the enterprising person to want to do everything to make sure it is done. However using other resources can be much more effective.

That is why property can be such a good long term strategy. The Buy to Let market has become 'overrated' and it may not necessarily be the perfect time to enter this market. However, property is an investment on which Banks will lend up to 85% of the funds. If the market is right and you can get a tenant, their rental (other peoples money again) will pay the mortgage, provide cash flow and hopefully lead to a capital gain, with very little input from you in terms of time.

It is also important for you to carefully guard your ideas. If you have intellectual property such as a patent or copyright you may be able to earn a financial return on its use.

I am suggesting you do this with the utmost integrity. There have been companies and politicians who have achieved wealth through the use of their country's resources, However use the leverage of others, ideally on a win/win basis, or you will find that other people will simply use your time to leverage their own projects, whether in business or within an organisation.

Taxes

Taxes can be a very substantial drain on your ability to build your wealth portfolio. However in most countries tax is the key source of government income and it is the law that you pay your share. I am certainly not recommending evasion which is against the law. Tax avoidance where you plan your financial affairs in an attempt to at lessen tax liabilities is worth consideration. Let us say that you have written a book for which you have been offered a contract worth £80,000. The book has taken you five years to write and your probably won't write another one. This £80,000 is a 'one off' lump sum which could prove to be a substantial part of your investment portfolio and long term retirement income. It is perfectly reasonable to plan to limit your tax liability. For instance it is possible to operate within a company, and hence be eligible for a substantial tax deductible, self administered tax fund payment.

Plan for Tax

If you are self employed you need to decide to plan ahead for tax, in order to get yourself the best deal possible without breaking the law. Limited companies can be very advantageous tax vehicles for growth businesses.

I don't want you to get obsessed about tax.

For employees there can be significant tax advantages in having a part time business which could claim expenses and provide potential tax rebate situations.

The important thing with tax is to be strategic. Before making any financial decision you should have a review with your tax adviser.

As an enterprising individual with financial skills, you will always consider the tax angle as part of your decision.

However if you want to be based in UK or USA you will have some tax liability and you need to accept that the most important thing to do financially, is to determine your margin and ensure that you get paid. Getting used to setting aside 25% of the profits for tax provision is a good habit to encourage.

Ratios

One of the key tools any business person has to consider are business ratios. These are a set of statistics based on financial statements. We have already talked about some of them, gross margin on sales, net margin etc. If you can understand Balance Sheets and profit, you can measure the return on the worth of your business. Let us say your business balance sheet shows a bottom line figure of £100,000 but it only earns you £5000 per year That is not a good return on your investment.

Financial decisions financially depend on the use of ratios. If you buy a property for instance, which may look very desirable, or which is in Spain in your favourite holiday destination, what is important is whether the deal makes financial sense. What did you pay compared to its market value?

When you add up all the costs and compare these to your financial return adjusted for periods without a tenant, is it still a good deal? If it isn't, walk away from it... Business is a numbers game. If you only look at one deal or one customer you tie yourself in. If you want to buy or start a business, you should look at least 100 possibilities until you see the right business or right deal for you. The same applies to looking for a job.

The Person You Are

The fascinating thing that I have discovered through working in a bank or as an accountant is that it is the habits which you have, rather than your income which matter. You frequently encounter see people who earn £60,000 per year, and who spend £62,000, and people earning £10,000 a year who save £2,000 per year they can use to invest in the purchase of commercial property.

You might dismiss this chapter as the ramblings of a boring accountant, (and you may be right)! What I want to do is save you from some of the financial heartache I have experienced, not because I didn't have financial qualifications, I became a qualified accountant and financial planner, but because having qualifications does not guarantee that you have the competences and will act in the best way for yourself. A lot of the points I am making come from financial mistakes I personally made.

Be clear what you want to do financially. Do you want to be wealthy? If so at what level?   What lifestyle do you want?   Do you have the right plan to get what you want?

Pick your own business, or simply take the example of where you currently work. What will you have to do to be financially independent in 10 years? Email your plan. What financial changes do you need to make?

Like all the E Factors, there is no better learning place than in the game of life. The next time you have a financial decision to make look, at it differently.

My advice is to make money and use it wisely for your own freedom, your family and to help the community.

As one famous business person said "once you get money out of the way then you can be good." Get it out of the way by treating it with respect, and make sure you have the strategies to make it help you do what you want to do with your life.

We never found out what happened to the new scrooge in 'A Christmas Carol' after he began to treat people well, and to helping others. That did not make him a fool. Wealth and the ability to handle money; whether as a business person or manager is a key requisite of the job to enable you to enjoy your life in this commercial world.

TASK

Pick your own business, or simply take the example of where you currently work. What will you have to do to be financially independent in 10 years? Email your plan. What financial changes do you need to make?

CHAPTER SIX

INFLUENCE

INFLUENCE

It is important to realise that none of your business career or life plans will come to fruition, unless you get other people to support your ideas. You need to convince other people that your ideas/projects will work and that you are the person who can deliver these successfully. Therefore, you need to influence/persuade others to back you. Influencing consists of a number of individual skills which we will examine, all of which are important in delivering results:

Communication skills
Networking skills
Selling/negotiating skills

Unfortunately like many of the other enterprise skills, you are not taught these in any standard school or university course. However you can acquire them if you are prepared to learn the basic transferable skills but above all to apply and practice them in your every day life.

Communication

Are you a good communicator? Other people need to be aware of your ideas/projects and you need to interact to make things happen. However there is more to communication than simply speaking or writing.

The fact is that you are always communicating whether you realise it or not. You communicate non – verbally as well as verbally and unless you get it right you are unlikely to be as effective a communicator as you could be.

Your body language; your tonality; what you do; what you wear; all communicate a message to others. We will discuss this again, when we talk about personal branding.

Be a Listener

Ironically although we are trying to help you get better at getting your ideas across to persuade other people, one of the key skills is to genuinely take time to listen to other people; as Covey says "to understand before being understood".

This doesn't mean pretending to be interested, it means taking the time to understand where the other person is coming from, whether you agree with them or not. Everyone has a story to tell and a point to make. You will defuse arguments, and have a better chance of persuading others if you respect other people and their viewpoints.

Do it with sincerity or don't do it at all. I'm not saying that if you are at a party and you are cornered by the party 'bore' you have to sit there in rapt attention for hours on end. However be interested in others and what they have to say. You never know what you might learn!

Students, who go for management assessment job interviews with the large corporations, often try to get their point across by 'bossing' the group. What they don't realise is that the students who listen to others and understand where the group is going before they say anything are noticed by the interviewers. They are seen as having the best potential. Listening is a key skill. You need to understand your customer, friend, supplier or family member, and their priorities before you attempt to gain their support or influence.

Remember however, sincerity is everything both in learning and in communication.

Now are you listening?

The Mix

Research suggests that Communication consists of 5% words, 40% body language and 55% tonality. People pick up on your non verbal communication. Does what you do, your body language and your tonality all give the same message?

For instance I met an old acquaintance this morning in a coffee shop. I asked him how he was keeping and what he was doing. He said he was freelancing and looking about for the right position. However his flat tonality, lack of enthusiasm and poor posture/body movement told me he was in bad form, and that things were not going too well. Am I a mind reader? Unfortunately not. That was simply the message he was giving me, unintentionally or not. I could have put some work his way but the message I got was of someone in turmoil, not ready to undertake the project work I needed done.

Physiology

One Israeli psychologist has suggested that there is a strong link between mind/body, and that how you move can improve your 'state'. If you stand up straight, look ahead and move energetically, your mood will improve.

Try it! Do you feel any better?

Let's say you are going in to meet your Bank Manager to seek funds for your new business. If you move confidently, have good posture and give off a relaxed yet confident and business like demeanour, he/she will take you more seriously. What the bank tries to assess is whether you believe in your project, and how you will react to pressure. Obviously in this kind of interview situation, it is easy to feel nervous and give off anything but positive vibes. However there is a secret. By behaving confidently you will convince yourself and by feeling more confident will become the enterprising person the Bank Manager is looking for.

One person who impressed me recently was a contestant on 'Dragons Den' which is a television programme which focuses on would be business people pitching their idea to a panel of multimillionaires prepared to consider investing in their idea. The panel usually start off by attacking both the ideas and indeed the contests, which clearly makes for compulsive viewing. However one very quiet young lady whose business idea related to fashion jewellery, impressed me by both her ability to listen to the panels criticisms and also by her relaxed yet confident manner. She stood confidently, listened respectfully and responded not with aggression but with quiet assurance, and her voice, posture and words demonstrated both self belief and a willingness to listen to other points of view.

The panel got the message! They all respected her influencing skills and she successfully secured a major investment in her business.

Tonality

Tonality refers to more than just the pitch or timbre of your voice, important though that is important as it often reflects the subtle message behind the words spoken or written.

Many of us use emails or texts nowadays for quick communication. Sometimes however communication by email delivers the wrong underlying message.

As you can imagine, whether in face to face discussions or in telephone conversations, voice tonality can play a very important part. One of the key weaknesses many people have is a lack of variety in their tonality. Vary it! Make sure that you put enthusiasm in your voice and that the tonality above all represents what you feel. We all know the feeling that someone for instance has been "cool" to us over the phone, not because of the words they use, but by the tonality in their voice. Never underestimate the part it can play. Get it wrong and you can significantly dilute the success of your communication. A potential customer whom you are trying to convince of the contribution tour product can make to his business, will search for any sign that you do not believe what you are saying. The voice tone can give that message.

Communication Styles

To communicate successfully the most important thing is to be flexible. Different styles of communication are appropriate for different situations and for different people. You may think "I talk very enthusiastically and if they don't get the message that is their fault" but it is important to take your time, assess what is appropriate in each situation, and respond accordingly.

Respect for other people means that it is important to convey your message in a way that they will understand. As Richard Bandler a famous communication specialist has said "the meaning of communication is the response you get". So the responsibility is yours. Some people like "the big picture", some like the detail. Your job as an influencer is to satisfy everyone.

Sensory Systems

Neuro-Linguistic Programming (NLP) which is one of the most popular communications models works on the basis that everyone has a different view of the world. Some people are visual and look for visual evidence to understand everything. Some are auditory who emphasise what they hear, while some rely on their feelings and like to touch physical evidence.

influence

People also use language related to their own sensory system. Visual people talk about "getting the picture" Auditory like "the sound of things" and for kinaesthetic people things "feel right". Visual people often speak quickly in a high pitch voice and are obviously into how things look, including their physical appearance; auditory have great tonality in their voice and kinaesthetics speak slowly focusing on their feelings. Start listening to peoples' language and try to identify what they prefer.

Very interesting you may say but so what? The danger is that if you are dealing with someone who has a primary sensory system which you have not accurately identified, each of you could end up talking at different speeds and using different words to mean the same thing during your conversation. This is hardly likely to improve the communication process.

Let us say you are a 'feelings' person presenting your findings on a project to your 'visual' boss. You keep explaining how you have a 'good gut feeling about the project'. You speak slowly and talk about "grasping the opportunity". Your 'visual' boss however may well become impatient with your slow rate of speech and interrupt to ask "what the big picture is". He comments that your power point slides are not colourful enough. This is a classic process of miscommunication.

A good communicator who is preparing a speech sets out to work on visuals, adding sounds, working on their words and emphasis and giving out detailed handouts for the kinaesthetics to grasp. He/she will employ all three types of language, and if presenting to one key individual will do his/her best to focus on their preferred system. Are they being calculating? Surely you should just be yourself and people should take you as they find you? NO! That is a haphazard approach. To communicate effectively it is vital to get the message across and minimise the barriers to clear communication between both parties.

EXERCISE

Listen to the words people use. What is important to them? What do you notice?

The Outcome formula

With any communication be clear as to what outcome you want to achieve. Learn to carefully assess both verbal and non verbal signs as to whether you are getting what you want and adapt your style or method.

Rapport

A key part of what you are doing here is building rapport. This does not mean pretending to be someone's best friend or faking an interest in something you are not interested in. It involves trying to be sensitive so that the person you are talking to feels a sense of affinity with your views and is prepared to talk to you even if you are in an adversarial position. It often helps to try to identify peoples' sensory system, and trying to match breathing, tonality and body posture in a subtle way.

Let me give you an example of this. A very angry customer is on the phone. They complain loudly that "this is the second time your company has let me down". Conventional customer services wisdom insists that you quietly calm them down.

However first of all you have to match their breathing and speech tonality otherwise they may simply become angrier. This doesn't mean that you shout loudly at them, but it is important to match them to gain some rapport before you gradually edge towards a solution. Try it and see. I found this out by an accident with an aggressive client who never seemed to respond to my calming measures. He found out my home number and rang me on a Friday night about a fairly minor problem. As usual he was sounding off. Unfortunately (or fortunately as it turned out) I answered his rather aggressive communication style in similar vein, simply because at 10 o'clock on a Friday night I could not be bothered to get into "calming down" mode. To my surprise I built a much more effective rapport with my client than before which continues to this day.

The basis of rapport is that people communicate better with people who are like them. That does not mean that you pretend to like people you don't. However if you need to communicate effectively with anyone it is better to "be on the same wavelength". It is important to show respect for how they communicate.

This can include their style of presentation, the words they use, non verbal clues, body language and even their cultural background.

Some people – quite often the successful ones – do this effortlessly. You can do it too, and you will improve the effectiveness of your communication, if you practice rapport building.

EXERCISE

Go into a pub or restaurant watch groups of friends and couples. Look for any signs of rapport
Think of a difficult meeting you have coming up. Do a rapport plan with that person or group
Practice building rapport on a daily basis. Be careful though, you may become too popular!

If you want to influence people you must build rapport before you attempt to influence/persuade them. The absence of any rapport will lead others to refuse to consider your point of view
These skills need to be used with the best of intentions. If you use them you will suddenly find a whole new world opening up to you.

Networking

The idea of deliberately meeting people socially with the prime purpose of advancing your career or business does not sit easily with many people. If it is done with the intention of using other people solely for your own ends, that is indeed shallow. However building contacts who will be of help to you can be a fun process and should be an ongoing part of your business and personal life. If you are totally antisocial and refuse to speak to anyone other than a few close friends, you may get some 'brownie points' – but unless you are either vastly wealthy or hold some position of power, you will be neither a business nor a social success. It is an old truism but one which you must take onboard "it is not always what you know but who you know".

This section sets out to improve your personal ability to achieve results. I know in an ideal world these results should be based solely on your abilities and hard work. Sadly that is not always the case. If you are really incompetent at your job or your business does not add value, your networks will not save you. However they will provide significant advantages to anyone willing to work at networking in a continuous systematic way.

Why are Networks So Useful?

Networks are firstly great fun. They will help you will gain understanding in a wide variety of areas. You will also be able to access a lot of informal information that would not reach you otherwise. Last but not least you will also know a lot of people who know people who know people who could make a huge difference to the outcome of your project. This reflects something known as "the power of 6" which is the concept that everyone in the world is only six people removed from anyone else through the power of networking.

In other words your network can reach out worldwide through this process of geometric progression.

Let us say you have 5 key contacts who also each have 5 and so on. This gives 5 levels 5x5x5x5x5 = 3125 people, and illustrates the value of being 'well networked' so that your 'social capital' can be actually an asset. Of course it is not always the quantity of your contacts but the quality. It clearly makes a difference if you have some 'key influencers'.

Unfortunately what this sometimes means is that at business or social events people make a beeline for those who are perceived to be successful either in monetary terms or in terms of their 'clout'.

It is much better to be more relaxed and talk to everyone there. There is no point going if all you do is talk to the friends you came with.

Hopefully the new people you meet, even if they are unlikely to directly present you with any business opportunity, will most certainly know someone who will. However it is important to remember that people pick up quickly on insincerity or those who will only talk to perceived 'heavy hitters'.

influence

Bad Networking

One of the worst examples of networking I came across was in USA. I was on an Entrepreneurship course and an evening event was held to teach us 'how to network the American way'.

Many net workers either told us their life story or very quickly moved on when they realised we could not provide venture capital or whatever their most significant requirement was.

The course leader was approached by a delegate, a medium ranking development officer whilst he was already speaking to a senior ranking aerospace delegate. As he shook hands he actually looked away from the development officer and continued his conversation with the Aerospace 'heavy hitter'. This is the type of networking which turns people off. You are there to meet people! If you do not show sincerity or respect for them you will create what is known as a 'negative networking syndrome'. Bad news spreads twice as quickly as good news as the story above illustrates – perhaps a salient lesson in the case of the circumstances outlined here!

How to Network

Always aim to meet at least two new people in any networking event. Inevitably, having made new contacts one common reaction is to look immediately for ways to 'use them' to move your career/business forward. This 'using' of people makes many people avoid the concept of making new contacts.

However once you have met someone who you have found interesting, it is invaluable to 'keep in touch' and look for any way in which you can be of assistance to them. If you take this attitude you should be setting up a network capable of giving and receiving in an ethical way.

Be Organised

The consequences of not being organised can negate the advantages of creating a strong network. You need to keep in touch with your network otherwise it will simply die. Making contact is only 'half the battle', keeping in contact is very important. Set un-ambitious but achievable targets to keep in touch with your network.

Let me give you an example of how not to do it, again from my own repertoire. As a young ambitious consultant I was making contacts looking for key referral business. One enterprise agency manager in particular sent me 40 new clients in the first six months, a godsend for my business.

I really liked him and enjoyed spending time in his company. I became so busy that I didn't manage to see him for a year, on the basis that having a cup of coffee with him was not 'chargeable time'. As a result I lost touch with a person I liked and respected. He also did not refer any more business to me, not because of any fall out, but simply because we were not in touch at times when he was referring a client. I was no longer the first name to spring to mind. A salutary lesson!

Objectives

You should aim to meet at least three new people a week in connection with your business. Your job is to keep in touch with them on a planned basis.

Networking Plan

For some of you, networking will come easily; some of you may already be blessed with a network through family contacts. However whatever the state of your network work at it.

The keys are:
network on an ongoing basis
keep in touch
try to help at least one person in your network every week

Silverman, a Marketing Guru in USA claims that networking is the number one marketing strategy for all companies. The reality is that your network will at times be the difference between success and failure in business. You have to find the right balance and go after it in a structured fashion. Set outcomes, review your performance at networking events and learn from great net workers. However do it in a relaxed fashion. If you are too focused on an immediate business return, people will feel used and the benefits both directly and indirectly will be significantly lower. Be sincere and search continuously for interesting ways to help and connect with your networks.

EXERCISE

Plan your next networking event. Send your record of a weeks networking activity together with your own reflections to info@efactor.eu – Lets Network!

Sales

Introduction

The concept of selling is sadly an alien word to many people who want to be enterprising, start businesses or make projects happen.

Many people see "selling" as some type of socially unacceptable activity where people are sold something they don't want or need by someone who "cons" them into it. People spend their whole life avoiding this activity. However this need not be the case. As Robert Louis Stevenson said "everyone is selling something all the time".

If selling means persuading someone to buy a product/service or idea, then everyone does do it. Any form of selling activity should be based on market research and promotional activity. In general to attempt to persuade someone to buy something they don't want or need is a waste of time and very inefficient.

However even with a properly targeted audience, you still have to persuade people to buy or support your project. You will need to sell yourself to your prospective boyfriend/girlfriend, his/her parents, prospective employer and a Bank Manager for money. The list is endless. Persuasive communication is one of the key transferable skills essential to all of us regardless of whether we work in a business or own it.

If you decide to work in the Charitable sector you will need to persuade potential sponsors to back you, persuade your chosen target group to use the charity and influence volunteers to commit time and effort to your project.

The basic premise of this section is therefore that everyone should attend a sales course. Forget the view that we have been programmed to avoid the "S" word.

At one Management Development programme in London one of the English participants asked what my area of research was and how I was applying the business model we were working on. I explained that I was applying it to sales. Unfortunately being of Northern Irish extraction I pronounce my vowels rather differently from someone born in England. My new friend thought I was working with 'seals' and was therefore a zoo keeper or circus performer. This conversation continued for three days until he asked me if I had worked with any other animals.

Eventually we both realised that we had been talking about different things. However I sometimes do believe that people would rather work with 'seals' rather than learn how to make "sales".

Learn the skills and use them appropriately and ethically. Much of what you achieve in life will be based on deals you make with family and friends as well as with business associates. Until the other party agrees to back your proposal nothing can happen. Persuade and influence in an ethical way or leave everything to chance!
It is your choice.

Selling is a Process.

There are several stages to every successful sales/influence process. This section will analyse each consecutive stage and suggest which behaviours to adapt or learn.

Do Your Homework

It is important to remember that you are trying to do a deal with someone in a position to make a final decision and who is potentially interested in talking to you.

Undertake your market research and do not waste your time in targeting the wrong market/audience for your product or service. Failure to take this first step, together with the attitude that you should 'sell your product to anyone you can find whether they are interested or not' is a basic cause of the jaundiced view of selling we have noted above. Perseverance is a strong quality but hounding people who do not want to know is unethical as well as wasting valuable time.

Prospecting

Qualify your prospects. One of the key ways of ensuring you only deal with people who are potentially interested is to build in a steady flow of 'prospects' that you can work with on a relaxed basis. You don't then have to 'power hose' the one or two people you have found by chance and you can concentrate on finding the right mix of person versus product or service to make the sale and achieve both success and customer satisfaction.

How Do You Prospect?

First of all it is essential to find out as much as possible about your potential customer. Let us say your ideal customer is a woman 25–35 with a child under 5 and with a family income of £35000. Where do they live? What do they spend money on? Where do they shop?

You need to develop a system to make them aware of what you have to offer. This means adopting a variety of low cost strategies to create enquiries.

Use six or seven different strategies. If these are then are targeted at an audience who clearly need the benefits of your products you can reasonably expect a number of enquiries about your products.

It is essential however to do this on a regular basis in order to ensure that you never run out of potential customers.

Many people, be it someone starting a business or someone looking to get potential members to their new club stop prospecting the minute they think they have 'enough' business or enquiries for their project.

It is essential to keep trying to convert expressions of interest into sales or deals, and it is always helpful to play a numbers game.

One simple such game/ rule of thumb to adopt is that you need ten enquiries to get an appointment and ten appointments to get a sale.

Relax Not Everyone Will Buy

If there is one crucial lesson to learn from this section, it is that not everyone will buy from you, even though your market research has shown them to be an interested customer.

Yet many of us are sensitive souls at heart. If we talk to someone about our project and they do not give us a positive response, we take it personally.

I used to run a programme for women entrepreneurs. Many excellent graduates attended this course. They all had good ideas, and worked hard at developing their business. Unfortunately when most of them were unsuccessful in making their first sale they were devastated, and many of their businesses did not develop any further.

Listen and Ask Questions

We have already mentioned the importance of listening, and this is a key skill in persuading others. Listen to what they say and look for signs in their tonality or body language, which indicate their key areas of concern.

To get the right information ask questions to get their reaction. Ask open questions which allow the potential customer to show their true motivation. It is essential to find out what their "hot button" is, what matters most to them and to try to decide whether you can provide solutions with your product/services. The big moment which tests your integrity is when you have listened to the needs of the potential client and find that your business does not offer an appropriate solution to their needs. Are you prepared to walk away, even though you desperately need the sale?

The answer is you must be. To build a relationship of trust with a customer you must act in their interests. This may well be difficult but remember, "Play fair today, get rich tomorrow!"

By developing a series of prospects as we outlined above, you can be more relaxed about who buys now.

Dealing with Objections/Closing

Welcome objections, it gives you the chance to deal with any potential problems.

You have also got to be prepared to 'close'. A classic example of someone not doing this was John Cleese when he played the part of a sales person calling on a stationery shop week after week and having cups of tea with the owner. One day a stranger appeared with forms to be signed and then left after five minutes. John Cleese innocently asks "who is that?" "Oh that's the man we buy our stationery from" was the reply.

What was the message? John Cleese represented all those people who make contacts with potential prospects, build a relationship but never actually ask for the business.

If you want to achieve results with your selling/presentations, you will have to ask for the business. It is a nice idea to think that once you have made contact with the 'customer' that they will offer you business, but you need to ask for what you want. Sir Alan Sugar of 'Apprentice' fame is very clear when advising would be Entrepreneurs that they need to ask clearly for what they want.

Part of this problem goes back to the fear of rejection. As part of the cultural bias against the concept of selling, some people will react rather inappropriately if they feel they are being sold to. You need to relax and realise that 'some will some won't.' So what next? Asking for the sale, yet being relaxed about the outcome is the key to success.

Closes

Some professional sales people will learn a variety of closes in order to 'trick' the customer into buying. You need to ask for the sale as part of the process and pick up on the signs where the customer still wants to buy and where he is wriggling out of it.

Like every negotiation the sale is only made when the contract is signed and money passes hands. It is vital to tie down the final details because it is the difference between getting the business or not.

Like all skills you will get better as you practice. Selling and personal influence are very similar and you ultimately are judged by the results you achieve. However you may learn more from the sales or negotiations you lose, than the ones you win. Take at least half an hour after every major 'pitch' to assess what you did right or wrong. If you have been interviewed for a job you have the right to ask for feedback. Gradually you will get better. It is not always obvious what you have done wrong and you may need to rely on informal feedback and non verbal signs.

A friend of mine who was being interviewed for a job as a teenager shut the door on the head of the second interviewer when walking nervously into the room. He didn't get the job; what a surprise! It is not always as obvious as this but if you learn from your mistakes you are less likely to make the same ones again.

AIDA

As we said earlier sales is a process. It is important that you do the right things in the right order.

AIDA is a mnemonic for

> Attention
> Interest
> Desire
> Action

This is the normal process you need to stage manage before you have a chance to make the sale.

Following this process will gradually build interest and lead to the opportunity for a decision.

A- Attention

Let's see how it works.

Whether doing a presentation at a job interview or doing a 'pitch' you need to get the attention of the people you are dealing with. Hopefully if you have done your homework before the meeting you will have an idea of the best way to attract the attention of your audience. What you are searching for is their 'hot button'; what will attract their interest. For instance if you were trying to sell a product and you know the company's main focus is on cutting costs, an opening remark like, "This product will save you £15,000 per annum" is likely to get you at least a fair hearing.

I - Interest

You need to get your audience interested.

Be clear and try to communicate in a meaningful way to attract and keep their interest.

Do everything possible to bring your presentation alive, use visuals, vary your voice – if it's a product have a sample.

Make sure your communication style is appropriate for your audience. If you are trying to 'sell' community service to teenagers you need to talk their language and build rapport in your presentations. Again being clear as to what you want to achieve is necessary. Excellent communicators will always be flexible and aware if their audience is losing interest.

D - Desire

Basically your audience will only want a solution if you can show that you can give them one of their main desires/benefits. By this stage you should have found out what they are and you need to show how you can meet these desires.

Equally if you can't genuinely meet one of the key desires/benefits, you should not pretend. Honesty at this stage will give you a strategic advantage with your potential customer in the long run.

A - Action

If you have got your client interested and have shown how you can solve their problems, the key is to now ask for the sale to see if they are prepared to take action. If they say "let me think about it" that means they are not ready. It is important to recognise what your client is really thinking and when they are looking for a way out if you are to avoid wasting your time.

Flexibility

Ultimately although you regularly follow the same process, how you behave must depend on what you are selling and who you are selling to.

It is useful to have a clearly thought through process and to organise each stage. However each company/person is different and it is important that you respect that difference. Some will need help in making a decision, some will not respond to any suggestion of an aggressive approach. Your ability to deal with a variety of audiences will depend on your competencies including belief, self confidence and ability to master your fears.

Perhaps the most important thing is to adapt your attitude to selling. It is a natural communication process and a vital life skill. If you are to achieve your goals you must influence other people to support your cause. The ability to do this with integrity can also make the difference as to whether a business deal is done, a community project is supported, or indeed whether a you get that job.

You have been learning a full range of enterprise skills. Basically an Entrepreneur finds an idea and makes it happen. To make any project happen you will need to convince a lot of people, suppliers, customers, banks and staff to support you and believe in your project. Your ability to influence them to support you will play a key role in the success or failure of your project. Influence or fail!

If you have few of these skills and no network you may feel you are not in a position to influence what happens.

However start where you are now, decide what decisions you need to influence, operate to a plan, and if you complete the tasks set you will gradually improve your ability to influence customers. You can do it if you start practicing these skills in everyday life. It's up to you!

Tasks

You have been asked to sell a new student health drink which cures hangovers. Prepare a 3 minute pitch. Create a short written plan then actually make the pitch to friends/family – ask for feedback. E-mail your written plan and reflections to info@efactor.eu

Look ahead over the next three months to where you need to persuade someone to support you. Create a sales plan. Practice delivering it. Then carry out the actual presentation. What did you learn? What can you do better?

List ten things you can improve to help your influencing skills.

Try to meet 3 new people every week who are important to your business. Email: info@efactor.eu once a month to confirm that you have done this.

Twice a week for the next month, find an opportunity to practice gaining new skills. Email me, tell me what you have learned.

Email me about your idea! Why should I back you?

Practice persuasion skills every day. Let me know how you got on. If you still want to improve email me and I will give you my full list of suggestions.

Go on make my day! Persuade me!

CHAPTER SEVEN

LEADERSHIP – TEAMWORK

LEADERSHIP – TEAMWORK

To be successful as a leader you need to work hard on your leadership and teambuilding skills. Whatever project you are involved in you need to use all the resources including yourself to make it happen. This will include buildings and finance but above all people. Leadership is not management. You need to inspire teams to complete the projects, striving at all times to be the best you can be. Leadership is your capacity to turn a vision into reality.

Leaders Are Congruent

To be a leader you need to develop several of the E Factors as part of your behavioural make up. You need to be able to take action, to know what your markets are, understand business issues, have confidence and personal control, and the ability to influence others to follow your leadership and for your team to be able to make any project a success.

You will be better equipped with some of the E Factors than others, but if you want your team to be innovative, to develop individually you need to lead by example and show them that you are personally dedicated to the principles you are asking them to follow. In other words "walk your talk". Are you paying lip service to the ideas of the new project or are you dedicated and prepared to work together with your team?

Belief

Part of your objective as a leader is to demonstrate that you have belief in your vision. Not only do you have to deal with your own doubts you must inspire others by the power of your belief to take action to achieve the vision. Your belief should not waver (at least in public) until the project is successfully completed.

Vision

You should have a clear strategic vision of where you want you and your team to end up. Can you see the outcome of your project clearly? Can you see it happening? Can you think strategically beyond where you are now? How do you get better at this? Practice visualising your long term goals and the strategic aims of your organisation.

Team Player

As a leader you need to show that you are also a team player. You may need to lead the team but you need to be integrated with them and be able to work within the dynamics of the business to use the power of the team to realise your objectives.

Inspire

You must inspire others to join your team, and as part of your company to be able to take action. Your belief will enable you to do that, but you need to motivate the others, and to give them belief that the project will succeed. Your ability to achieve and retain their commitment to your business will make a significant contribution to your ultimate success.

Flexible

Flexibility is one of the key qualities of the entrepreneur. You need to know when to inspire, when to allow the team to get on with it, and when you must intervene to deal with a major problem. Although most theorists now favour this team based leadership approach, your style of leadership may need to vary according to the type of organisation you are leading, the type of project and the type of people involved.

Many leaders adopt one leadership style which is successful for say 70% of the time, but it is important to be able to adapt your style to changes in circumstances or personnel.

Know what you want. If you as a leader do not know where you want to end up, what chance does anyone else have? Take action and be able to measure whether you are achieving the outcome you need at each stage of the project. An ability to change strategy in response to changing circumstances is the mark of the good leader.

leadership – teamwork

Delegate

As a leader it is essential to be aware of the details of your business but you cannot afford to get bogged down in the day to day details. Leaders need to find others who are able to deal with these thereby clearing their own time to enable them to focus on strategic issues.

Face the 20% That Cause the Problems

In running any business project among the many things requiring attention there are invariably certain key issues, such as confrontations with troublemakers or difficult decisions to make, which are likely to cause problems. You should not delegate responsibility for these issues. They are the responsibility of a leader! It is these key activities which can make the difference between success and failure and where a leader can 'make their mark'.

The Ability to Think Perceptually

When you are making decisions about the future of your company, it is important to be able to remain aware of customer, staff and other stakeholder viewpoints. The ability to gauge any changes in these is the mark of a good leader.

Break Things Down

In addition to sharing your vision you need to be involved in the design of each step necessary to fulfil your vision, and aware of the obstacles which may emerge.

Find Managers Who Are Better Than You

When you recruit your team to take the business forward, look for people with special abilities. You may feel threatened by them but you need their expertise. Even if you are managing a small business start up, with all the lack of resources that this implies, look for key staff or external advisers who have the capacity to help you realise your vision. To employ people simply on the basis that they are less expensive to hire, demonstrates short term rather than strategic thinking.

Look For Communications Opportunities

Find new and creative ways to make things happen.

Rewards/Compensations

Give people a vested interest in the business as a way to ensure their long term commitment. You can also use short term celebration opportunities as flexible opportunities to reward people, and make sure that you show your appreciation in unexpected ways.

Clear Up the Leadership/Management Distribution

It is your job to create values and to design how your plan will develop but you will need the help of management to make things happen. You should only make decisions once you have sought expert advice. Your auditors or business consultants may give sound advice about how to run the business, but you as leader must take the decisions, using their advice to help you make your decision.

Everything You Do Matters

As a leader you are responsible for establishing and developing your organisational culture. If you are a poor time keeper, don't carry out promises (or threats) to punish others into do the same. Lead by example.

I have worked for organisations where the leader was very negative, was into micromanagement, and tended to have people similar to himself in positions of control. Needless to say that was not a highly motivating environment. I have also worked for organisations where the leader had a vision that inspired you and made you want to be part of the team that brought about the impossible.

Tough but Fair

I fully support the collaborative leadership model where achievements are very much a team effort. However staff are only human, and may well feel if you appear to be too "nice", that they can "push their luck". If you have good information and communication systems however, you will hear through the "grapevine" where this is happening, especially where these activities conflict with your mission. It is unwise however to overreact to small issues. However rest assured that if one of your managers has done something of which you don't approve, it can quickly become a habit, and you may end up with a much more significant problem.

Leaders are Listeners/Readers

You should always look for formal and informal information, and listen to feed back from sources both external and internal to your business.

Leaders are Creative

Your ability to solve strategic problems creatively is important, as is the way you react to the pace of innovation. You should be open to new ways of doing things because the right innovation can significantly improve your business.

Leaders Like to Learn

I am constantly amazed by the leaders of growing and large companies who are keen to learn, build clusters and to network with other Chief Executives. They may have achieved conventional success but they are constantly looking for one or two new ideas from their competitors which will make a difference to their own business.

Coaching

I see coaching from two angles. Firstly as a leader you should be able to coach others in order to motivate them and provide the springboard for them to achieve high performance. Your job is to listen to your team to facilitate the development of your key objectives.

The difficult question is "who coaches the coach?"

As a leader you may be in a position where you report to the Board of Directors or to Shareholders and there is no one to act as your mentor. You need someone who is not involved in day to day decisions and who is able to help facilitate your decision making. Finding an effective coach is a worthwhile investment. This facilitation will enable you to set out your goals and have someone act as a sounding board to motivate, encourage and help you without being directly involved in your career.

Respect others style

It is important that you should be able to work with a variety of senior people who may have different styles. You need to develop your ability to create rapport with them all, and to improve your capacity to create group rapport when you all meet.

Trust

Creating a climate of trust and integrity is your job. You need to earn trust and respect rather than expect it because of your position. How you behave will ultimately decide whether your team trusts you and will work effectively and constructively with you.

TASK

Are you a leader? What is your vision of your organisations future?

Learn From Models

There are many people who have successfully created a transformation within organisations large and small, private and public. Read their books, network with them, watch what they do. Copy their behaviour – it works!

Values

It is up to you to impose business values from the top. Those values might include things such as customer service or integrity. You need to set them out in a way which makes it very clear that you expect everyone to accept them and to incorporate them into their contributions to your business.

leadership – teamwork

Your Personal Leadership Style

Are you clear what your personal leadership style is? How can you enrich? How can you improve? You should attempt to acquire behavioural skills which will achieve the rewards of good leadership. Identify any weaknesses in your style. Can you remedy any competencies where you may be deficient? Let us say you have been a successful small business owner, but you are now a senior leader in a public sector organisation. How have you adapted your behaviour to be the best leader possible in your new position?

TASK

Name a leader that you admire — why?

Confidence

It is essential that you are both confident and well organised. You may not always feel confident about yourself or your business,but your influence is important for all your stakeholders. Your confidence will be infectious but so also will an obvious lack of confidence, and your style will influence whatever the organisation does.

You need to be able to command respect and to ensure that you get both feedback and action from your staff.

How Do You Motivate Your Team?

You must make people feel that they are part of a team and offer them opportunities for advancement to fulfil their own ambitions within your organisation. This means that it is important to take time to listen to key individuals and to watch their non verbal language as well as their words, to enable you to assess what is really important to them.

State Management

Your ability to control your state and focus is vital, as particularly in times of crisis your team will look to you for the way forward. Your ability to appear calm, focused and in a powerful state will have a strong impact on how your organisation as a whole responds to change.

The ability to give your best performance when you really need to is important. The challenge you may have is to be able to work at your best at all times, rather than simply when you are under stress, or in a 'fire fighting' crisis. The better your performance as leader at the strategic level, the less fire fighting there will be.

You Will Use Planning and Creative Models

An important part of your job is to plan the future of your organisation. You need to have the capacity to see creative possibilities, allow others or yourself to suggest new ideas and then to be able to disassociate yourself and take a critical view to iron out any practical difficulties.

Overcome Limiting Beliefs

A key challenge will be to overcome the limiting beliefs of other key employees in your organisation. It is essential that you understand their perspective, respect it and are able to find a way to gradually win them to your way of thinking. This may include achieving small targets and building trust and belief step by step. The key is to get others to act thoughtfully in every situation, even if they believe practically that their choice of actions is limited.

The Right Message

We have mentioned what an important part communication plays in leadership. The worry is that other key players may get the wrong message. Miscommunication can cause real difficulties. You need to consider carefully how best to communicate in order to achieve the clarity that is needed. Communication and persuasion will play an important part in your leadership style.

Learning

Your ability to lead the group will be influenced by your own beliefs and functions. Being aware of this is 'half the battle'. You also need

leadership – teamwork

to be able to identify what is required and when it is required. Sometimes you will need your team to develop new ideas, which may require a lot of stimulation by yourself.

Particular Leadership Skills

This book has already indicated a number of leadership skills which you can develop. It is not enough to know that you should show strong belief. This is a behaviour/skill that you must practice in order to be able to convince your stakeholders that you are a 'born leader'. The skills are listed below:

Personal Mastery

Establish a vision and a set of interim steps to implement that vision. Keep yourself, your goals, and your personal states aligned to your mission..
Practice building your belief to achieve your mission.
Work on your flexibility in your leadership style, and your ability to influence.

Working with Others

It is essential to realise that different people do think differently. You need to win over those who are against the changes which you want, and you need to overcome resistance to change by whatever method works best in any given situation. Your respect, ability to listen, to build rapport and to put yourself in the position of anyone who opposes your proposed changes provides a good basis for your campaign of influencing your opponents. Always remain aware of the impact which different styles have on different people, and on their perceptions both of the problems and of the level of change required.

Skills Requirement

You need to build your own motivation and to be able to communicate as effectively as possible. At times you will need to work not only on your own tasks but on those you need to influence. Unless you match your mission with other peoples' values, or get them to change their values you will encounter strong resistance to change.

Sporting Heroes

I realise that some of you love sport, but it may be of little interest to others. However sporting leaders do behave in many of the ways we have outlined and are seen by some people as great role models. Stephen Gerrard, who is captain of Liverpool Football Club is one good example At half time in the 2005 final of the Champions League, his team were losing 3 - 0 to AC Milan who were the hot favourites to win the trophy. Somehow Gerrard and Rafael Benitez (the club manager) 'turned things around'. During the half time break Benitez remained very calm and in control. He did not speak of victory but of taking a first step by scoring a goal within the first ten minutes of the second period which would reduce their deficit. He also changed his team's tactics having realised that his initial strategy had been unsuccessful. He also reminded the players to play to show their appreciation to the fans, all 42000 of them who had travelled to Istanbul and were singing the Liverpool anthem "you'll never walk alone" despite watching their team being humiliated in the first half. When Gerrard their leader on the pitch, responded with a fantastic goal, he then used all his belief to motivate the rest of the team to believe that they could do more. The rest is history. This is a wonderful practical example of belief, flexibility, action, and leadership linked to great teamwork.

It also illustrates the need to want to win, to finish the job. Over the period since that game, Benitez the Liverpool manager has demonstrated other leadership qualities by progressively selling some of the players in his squad, who although they 'over performed' in that one match, have proven incapable of operating at the same level on a consistent basis. This may seem to be ruthless, but for any project to develop successfully management need to be prepared to take tough decisions which will work strategically, but may often be very unpopular in the short term. Some people may find this difficult, particularly if they have excellent rapport with their existing team. Obviously people need to be treated fairly, but the mission is everything and sacrifices frequently have to be made.

In the area of business, there are many examples of leaders who have removed themselves from the chief executive role for the good of the organisation. Many entrepreneurs who possess the leadership qualities necessary to take a business through several growth stages may

leadership – teamwork

well decide to leave when the company becomes listed on the stock market. They are showing as leaders they realise their own skill base may be inappropriate for a company in this new environment, where relations with "the city" and corporate governance regulations become increasingly necessary.

Outside the worlds of sport and business there are also lots of examples of political leaders, locally and internationally, who have worked to a mission and made substantial progress in its achievement. However I think I will stay clear from citing examples here – this book is controversial enough!

Ethics

If a leader's ethics are suspect, this may well lead to a lack of ethics at all levels of the organisation. The ethical mindset of the leader should cascade down through the organisation.

Clear Communication

Everyone you deal with should be clear what you expect from them.

Promote Learning

You should encourage all staff to develop to the best of their ability. For some leaders this may be scary, a bit like bringing in highly talented individuals whose abilities you feel may surpass your own. Nevertheless bringing people in and looking for peak performance should be a value that sets your organisation apart from its competitors.

Decision Making

When the time comes you will have to make difficult decisions. How do you become an effective decision maker? Probably by making bad decisions, and learning from mistakes. An appreciation of all the key business dynamics including marketing, finance and people is important , as leaders who are specialist in one of these areas may tend to make a decision which focuses on his/her own specialist discipline to the exclusion of the others. For instance a leader with a marketing background might overlook strategic financial or people considerations in their decision making.

Energy

It may seem obvious, but it is still worth repeating that you need to have the energy essential to the successful management of change, and hence to the continued development of any project. Whatever the demands these activities make it is important to plan to have 'something left' for your private life, in order to maintain a constructive work/life balance.

The ability to relax no matter what the circumstances is useful, both because it helps in making detached, unemotional decisions in times of crisis, and because continuous stress saps energy and undermines the capacity to perform. Time spent with family or taking exercise will be time well spent even from a business perspective.

Admittedly, driving a project ahead in uncertain conditions can create its own adrenalin rush – which at times can be addictive. However many 'high performers' find it useful to take time off on a regular basis, simply because energy, relaxation, exercise and an life outside business can benefit both themselves and their business. Beware of being "busy" doing things that don't really make a difference to the end result. An hour wasted at the office is an hour you could have spent constructively either with your loved ones, or just enjoying life.

Risk Taking Decisions

One of the key lessons in entrepreneurship is that to be successful you must be a risk taker. This is also a valid proposition in public sector employment, for example when you are in charge of a new organisation such as the Child Support Agency you are taking a risk to some degree.

This does not mean in any sense to advocate the 'Gung-ho' ideal of a kamikaze pilot who dives in not caring about the consequence of decisions for anyone including themselves. Any new enterprise is a step into uncertainty. The best business plan in the world cannot guarantee a specific outcome. Even with the best laid plans you may well have to change direction and employ all your innovative skills to respond to uncertainty in a way which will keep your organisation developing successfully.

What separates the entrepreneur who is starting up a small business from the manager of a new company or a subsidiary in a large organisation is that the implications of corporate failure for the individual are direct and potentially more serious. Most small ventures are started with inadequate resources, with some capital at least provided by the founder. The owner will be personally liable for debts unless they operate under the protection of limited company status. Even with that protection however, they are likely to lose more financially than is the case of the corporate new venture manager. The latter will at worst lose their job and any potential bonuses, but provided the failure is not linked directly to their inadequacies he/she may be moved to a different role within the company.

A leader therefore is a risk taker, because they will often be instigating change and pursuing a strategic vision in an uncertain environment. However even the entrepreneur can reduce their risk to be a calculated one. One issue with your own venture, with no control from a holding company is that you are allowed / required to take all the decisions, regardless of your previous experience and it is only too easy to lose the power of detachment. A business can become an emotional attachment which many people hold on to well past its sell by date for reasons of ego, or because they want to maintain the business for staff or for the benefit of the community, even though the business model is no longer viable. So yes you do need to be a risk taker though the type and extent of the risk varies from project to project. The better you plan and utilise your E Factor Skills the better your chance of success.

A Good Leader Knows When To Go

A great skill can be to be able to follow Kenny Rodger's advice in the song "The Gambler" - "You got to know when to hold them, know when to fold them". Military leaders from time immemorial have learned to sense when the battle was definitely not going their way, and when to cut their losses to live to fight another day.

Decisions Under Uncertainty

Managers make decisions within definite operational structures. Leaders operate under uncertainty. You will gradually learn to develop the capacity to make decisions which clash with popular opinion but which make strategic sense. You need to be able to see the possibilities that others don't see.

Finally, you need to make decisions and then be prepared to implement an action plan immediately.

Learn From Your Mistakes

Sometimes you will call it wrong. A leader must take responsibility and be prepared to learn from a failure. A good leader knows that failure will inevitably happen from time to time, but will learn and if need be change strategy or if necessary timescales to achieve objectives.

Ultimately it is not sufficient to be able to simply 'drive your team' to develop to the best of their ability. It is equally essential, though often difficult to manage yourself in a way that enables you to focus on and maintain your inspirational role as a leader. You may occasionally feel as 'down' as your team and have to hide it from them. A determination to acting in a way which demonstrates that you continue to believe in your success will help, but always be yourself.

When I first went into business I had a set vision that a leader had to be loud, a great public speaker who aggressively motivated his team.

Having observed many leaders since then, I now realise that there are many different successful styles of leadership. Some leaders are quietly spoken, support their key players and lead mainly by example. They are persuasive and will lead by bringing the team along and will only take a different approach when there is a need for a change of strategy.

As the leader you set the agenda. You also set the culture of your organisation, and must demonstrate the kind of behaviour you expect from every member of your team.

Although there are many factors in total, being enterprising basically involves identifying an innovation or opportunity and making it happen through your leadership skills. Sometimes there won't be a large team within a small company, but even 'one person projects' will involve working with regional agencies, suppliers, customers,

leadership — teamwork

banks and business advisers. Your ability to lead them and make them all work to complete the mission will make the project succeed. Develop your own leadership style. Your main example may be someone who has operated in a different time, company or project. Learn from others but develop your own style based on your beliefs and strengths. Someone who can lead others need not have any particular technical knowledge, but must have the capacity to develop strategic vision and to 'make it happen'. Find opportunities to lead. Your ultimate potential will be realised when you develop as a leader, create a new project, and make it happen with a team. After that anything is possible.

TASK

In the next month find at least one opportunity to lead a project in business or the community. Make it a project that you are passionate about. Make it happen, learn along the way and above all have fun!

Teams

You will have noticed that in this chapter I have written about both leadership and teams. In my view the two areas are linked. A team needs to be led, and a leader will only have his vision realised through an excellent team. Many people who go into entrepreneurship start off with the concept of doing it alone. However any enterprise will benefit from group work and from the synergy that a good team can provide.

Team Development

Any team will take time to develop. There will be potential conflicts as everyone finds their roles at the start, and people often say that a team goes through the process of development, storming, norming, and performing. That is why a clever leader needs to be there to coach, facilitate and cajole as the team performs.

One of the problems which may well occur is the presence of someone on your team who does not really want to be there. Such people should be given every chance to get into alignment with all other members of the team. However if this fails it may be necessary for you to consider an exit route for them if they are not making a positive contribution to the team.

There is Room for Different Roles

Management development research suggests that the ideal team will have a mix of individuals with different strengths. Thus although an 'ideal' might seem to imply that everyone should have similar outlooks and skills, a team possessing a range of skills and outlooks will in practice perform more effectively, provided of course that they learn to work together as a team. Most teams need a leader / facilitator, who as a strong team player will always focus on team togetherness, someone who will raise alternative viewpoints and someone able to persuade people to take action. The key is the skills which individuals bring to the team. Ultimately of course each person needs to bring their own skills, plus an ability to respect the team and to want it to perform well.

Whatever its healthy differences, a team needs to share the same strategic mission. There has to be a compelling reason why they are together. That is what makes them a team.

The Purpose

Just as it is important for you to have a purpose, the group needs one too. It is particularly vital in the early stage when there will be some inevitable conflict, and also at a later stage when all the hard work has been done and the group may be finding it difficult to 'finish off' the project. Team members need to be able to ask and answer "Why are we here"? In many cases the 'why' is more compelling than the 'how'. I would suggest that you get your team together as early as possible and demand that everyone answer the question "why am I here?"

The group will no doubt have conflicting purposes and ideas but you need to find a common purpose. Until the purpose of the project matches that of the group, it will simply generate negativity.

leadership – teamwork

It will always be helpful if the group can be inspired or motivated at the earliest possible stage. While grandiose motivational speeches have their place, their effect may wear off only too easily.

At this stage the team also needs to create their values, and to set out a blue print showing how they propose to achieve their strategic goal.

A facilitator can be a great help in resolving conflicts, and in driving the agenda. The facilitator can also help to build the vision, to focus on beliefs and to challenge any negative beliefs which begin to surface.

Develop

Everyone in the team should have an agreed PDP (personal development plan). Team activities should be arranged to encourage team building. Everyone should understand roles other than their own. The use of rewards and recognition to show that the team appreciates each individual will also help them develop as a team.

Team Power

Although you may be the leader of the project you will obviously want to harness the power of the team. This means seeking out opportunities which allow other members to show leadership. A series of team tasks will help to make the team believe that they can get results together and will help build a sense of team morale. Each task should be designed to ensure that both individual members and the team as a whole are progressively 'stretched' as each task develops.

Be Positive

Always attempt to reward and recognise anyone who is acting for the good of the team, or are actively developing new behaviours.

Have fun. A team that plays together works together. This should not be forced, but a systematic series of fun events can change the team 'make up.'

I worked in one organisation where although we all mainly worked as consultants on individual projects, when we had fun days or evenings out every event seemed to create a potential team spirit. The only problem however was that there was a gap of a year between each event and we all went back out to own individual projects. Ironically most of us have now left the organisation and still get on well together. What a waste of group potential that was.

> **TASK**
>
> Think of a team project you were involved in. How did the team function? What role did you play? Was this the most suitable role?

Are You a Team Player or a Loner?

Many of you will start your own organisation because you want to run things your way. However your new business will need other people in areas such as Operations, Human Resource Management, Marketing and Accountancy as your business expands.

You may find this difficult, particularly if you have ignored the value of being a team player from the start. Much of the enterprise literature shows however, that the creation and building of a key team ethos, and a similar ethos within the company as a whole will play a strong role in your business development. Some of the most effective teambuilding activity I have seen done by entrepreneurs involves the development of a team able to turn their Bank Manager, Accountant, Lawyer and Business Advisers into an informal seamless team who work together on a number of projects. Once you may have set your project up it is important to listen to others and try to get the benefits of team synergy. Can you take on board the input of others or will you bulldoze them down? Business is a team sport and you must learn the skills.

People Skills

People skills play a vital part in developing any business. Can you give feedback to other team members? Can you motivate and

leadership – teamwork

encourage them for the good of the team? Can you show and give trust, and build rapport with other team members. A genuine interest in understanding the perspective of others is important. Honesty is vital but you need diplomatic skills particularly in the early stages to enable you to know how to get the best out of your team.

Group Brainstorming

As soon possible, get together a group of people from diverse backgrounds. Ask them to come up with ideas for a new project. Prepare to be surprised how a group can come together, and how their different perspectives can lead to the creation of a wide variety of ideas.

Have a Team Coach

It is useful to have someone who is not directly involved in the team to facilitate the group. Observation of how people perform in a group with individual feedback will help people adjust their behaviour. In many groups a real problem can develop where someone naturally dominates the group. This can de-motivate other team members and may even prevent them from taking part. Hopefully the group will bring such members into line, but at an early stage a facilitator might help.

TASK

Have a group meeting which you attend videoed. Get someone to observe and let the group watch the video. Who is open to learning?

Some entrepreneurs may be used to working on their own, and must learn to respect the group and realise that their behaviour must adapt in a group.

Original Individuals / Great?

Many people who do not contribute much as individuals, can, given the right group dynamic, make an effective contribution. It is all about achieving the Three Musketeers "one for all, all for one" attitude. People want to be valued and want to play their part.

I was recently involved in running an enterprise course. A number of students were randomly assigned to a group and had to complete a number of tasks over the period of a week. My role was to facilitate the groups. One group had everything: a very difficult individual who did not share the values of the rest of the group, a very strong minded dominant individual, and some people who were lacking in confidence. My role was not to tell the group what to do but at times to ask questions to help self awareness. The group went through some very difficult patches early on particularly with regard to consensus decision making. Gradually however, the group took some shape, and the difficult individual and the dominant one both became good team players. Again this followed the standard procedure – storm, norm, perform. The group found its own way to work. They were helped by having to complete a number of group tasks designed by the Belbin group, where physical tasks could only be completed by teamwork.

Belbin

Belbin developed a series of interesting psychometric tests designed to help provide information on how individuals perform in a group. The challenge is often obvious where you have a number of excellent individuals who all want to lead. In these circumstances there is likely to be conflict until a team consensus on leadership is found. One excellent lesson by participants on the course was the importance of being a team player. Many would – be entrepreneurs take time to understand the concept. Equally however the group has to guard against assuming the habits of an ineffective committee. It is essential to find someone who will keep them on course, and prevent the group from degenerating into a 'talking shop'.

> **TASK**
>
> Set up a small team to generate business ideas. Meet once a month for three months. Work to build a team. What did you learn? Would you have had more ideas as an individual?

leadership – teamwork

The Ski Trip

As we have already noted, it takes time to build a group. Many entrepreneurs will bring people in and then replace them immediately, as they try to find the 'right' individuals. The ideal is to give a new team a sense of achievable tasks and as momentum builds up, to 'really go for it'. On a recent ski trip I was able to observe and learn a lot about group activity. We were a variety of school parents thrown together for the trip. We were all beginners and all lacked confidence. As we went through the difficult early stages of learning to move on skis, and then tackle the more daunting tasks the activities were full of lessons for teamwork. Some of us who were falling less frequently than others initially became impatient with those who were taking longer to learn the skill. One individual admittedly quite fit, moved himself up a group to 'intermediate level' after the first day, so highly did he rate his performance. We did not miss his arrogant attitude towards the less talented skiers!

As well as learning individual ski skills the instructor focused on developing us as a group for a specific reason. We would eventually be going into tougher conditions in uncertain weather, and he knew that if anything went wrong we would need to stick together as a group.

He did take it to extremes. As I lost control of my skis and was heading down the slope out of control he advised "stay with the group David". Everyone thought it was hilarious and needless to say I learned the lesson. Gary, who was a bit of a daredevil kept heading off in the opposite direction to the group, and was constantly asked "where are you going Gary?"

I had great difficulty with the ski lifts particularly with the two main ones where you and your partner needed to stay balanced to keep it moving. However at the end of the week, we all as a group completed the ladies Olympic downhill. Those of us who were trying to individually excel had learned that supporting the group and having respect for everyone whatever their athletic ability, was more important than our own ego. The beer was good too! More team building!

Conclusion

A successful entrepreneur needs to learn to lead enterprises, but also must learn to be a team player. This applies not only to relationships with colleagues within your own company, but to a lot of external stakeholders. Collaborative relationships will ultimately prove much more successful if you have a "win/ win" approach. Learn to be a team player! Lead from the front and watch that project happen!

TASK

List the teams you work with. List three things you can do to build a team/collaborative framework.

---

leadership — teamwork

CHAPTER EIGHT

ACTION AND RESULTS

ACTION & RESULTS

Entrepreneurs or enterprising individuals are often 'outcome orientated', i.e. they constantly know what they are looking for strategically as well as in the present/immediate future. However without the capability to take action whenever it is required, you as an entrepreneur are unlikely to achieve any of your outcomes. Outcome/action orientation is a key enterprise competency and needs to be backed up by flexible behavioural patterns. However there are likely to be changes or reactions to actions already taken which may get in the way of achieving your targets. Your ability to identify feedback is crucial, whether it is verbal, written or accessed by more informal methods. If you are not getting the results you require you may need to adopt a different strategy.

This may seem obvious but you often find the sorts of individuals in the world of enterprise who push very hard but who at best get mediocre results because they do not observe the above rules. People who when they have an idea in their heads immediately go for it and take action without any thought to consequences or regarding what they actually want. This is better than no action at all, but is almost a "scattergun" approach one step forward and then one step back. You also get individuals who once they have devised a strategy act on it and will keep on doing so regardless of the consequences. The effect is a bit like keeping banging your head on a wall hoping it will break. I know it may depend on how hard your head is and how soft the wall is but the fact remains this is probably not very effective.

Why do they do this? Well if you are a disciple of positive thinking you will have developed a Churchillian response "never give up – never ever give up" Determination and persistence are valued qualities in someone starting an enterprise and rightly so. However there may be a need to adapt your strategy if it is not producing the results you thought.

You may also need to review your outcomes when something changes in your business model or changes the environment in ways that mean that your original outcome is no longer achievable. 'Outcome orientation' involves being clear about what you want at both macro and micro levels. If you are unclear as to what you want and where you are going to go, the environment will reflect back your uncertainty and you will produce mixed results.

Know What You Want

What do you want? Or as The Spice Girls said (sorry!) "tell me what you want, what you really really want". It is not always easy to know what you want particularly at a strategic level. You may be too busy passing exams, making a living and just getting by. Even worse you can often go into careers/relationships or even business agreements which are really based on someone else's wish list. A friend may propose a joint business venture; your father may have always wanted to be a Doctor and now wishes the same for you. That does not mean you take either option, unless it suits you. You can be open to other people's ideas. If you do not know what you want, either have your own plan or be part of someone else's.

How Do You Know What You Want?

You need to take some time out. It is good to start off with some "possibility thinking" as if there are no limits to what would you like to do, how much money would you like to earn? What contribution do you want to make? Assume you have no limits!

TASK

Take 5 minutes, write down as fast as you can without stopping anything you want to do or have in the next five years.

TASK

Look at your list; pick one long term and one short term goal. How much do you want them? Why do you want them? Write these goals out once a day.

action and results

The Most Vital Skill

You will see that "knowing what you want" is not as straightforward as you think, yet it is vital because you are setting out the direction of your future. Know where you are going and be able to measure it. There are very few limits to what you can achieve provided you have absolute clarity about what you want. It is important that you know where you want to end up in the long term as well as short term if you want to make sure you are on the right path.

Many goal setting specialists suggest thinking about where you want to be in ten years time. If you can visualise this, then work back from then, to identify each forward step. Try it now.

Your Purpose

Life can change at any time. Your goals may vary but it is useful to consider having a mission statement. A mission statement sets out clearly what you want to do to enable you to 'make a difference'. This may sound a little prosaic but it demonstrates that you have a purpose to use your talents and the abilities to help others. It provides a backstop/ support, if you are ever sidetracked.

Your purpose will usually include both doing what you love and what you are good at. If possible try to put your mission statement into one statement.

For example let's say you enjoy coaching business people by advising them and encouraging them to be successful.

Your mission statement could be "I want to inspire and motivate business people to perform at their best". Everything you do in life should be related to that mission.

The Why

It is important that your mission really motivates you and gives you a reason for taking action. If you are not passionate about it then it is simply not your mission statement. Many people are familiar with company mission statements which are often framed and displayed in the company's reception area. These by definition are someone else's mission and one that you may not feel passionate about.

Setting Out Your Mission

__TASK__

Name two of your talents

What are you good at and also really enjoy? Let us say you are an excellent teacher and you are very enthusiastic.

How Do You Enjoy Using These Skills?

When have you used the above qualities? Let us say you have been most enthusiastic when you have been teaching young children how to play tennis. They in turn loved your approach, made good progress and really enjoyed your lesson.

It would seem obvious that your purpose should be to teach tennis to kids. What we don't know however is whether there are other areas you would like to share with people. My suggestion would be that your mission statement would include sports coaching but expanded to include the general role of teaching.

"My mission is to teach others to be the best they can be using my enthusiasm and people skills. I teach business people and sports people of all ages to fulfil their potential and to have fun".

It is clear from this statement what you love doing as well as what you are good at. You may use various ways to harness that talent to help others but everything you do should be geared to teaching and working with people as it is clear that is what you love and what you are good at. When your purpose involves these two attributes it is much more likely that you will stick at it and will make a bigger contribution.

What Do You Want To Be?

Once you have sorted out your broad objectives, it is now time to be more specific. You will need courage to state this, because it will often seem as if the world makes the decisions about what you should be doing. Parents, friends, and workmates will all have pigeonholes into which they think you should slot, perhaps partly for your own good (as they see it) but perhaps unconsciously also to achieve some goal of their own.

Work on the Want List Again

Spend another ten minutes writing down everything you want. You might start off with a list of material possessions such as a castle, a Maserati etc, but somewhere in the list you will show what really is important to you, and what contribution you would like to make in life.

For instance let us say that when you go through your list, you find that sport is everything to you. It is the environment you within which you want to be work. A careers adviser would probably at this stage say "fine, that's your hobby. Now what work can you do to pay for that hobby"? Fortunately, if you want to work in sports even if you are an unlikely candidate to become a professional athlete, there are lots of other options available.

- sports agent
- sports coach
- sports lawyer
- physio
- sports finance
- run a leisure and sports complex
- become a sports journalist
- come up with a new product which could be used in your favourite sport
- sell sporting autographs
- become a sports psychologist

You can link your skills and enthusiasms to the area you love.

Where Are You Now?

People often find it difficult to identify where they are now, compared to where they want to get to. It is important to self assess and if need be get feedback from those around you. Don't fool yourself; there is no other place you can start, than where you are now.

Your Vision

Try to build a picture of your future. Visualise your job, career or business. What is your income? What type of people do you work with? What exercise do you take? The bigger the vision, the more you will believe it.

Spend ten minutes everyday going through that vision in the same detail.

It is important to know what you want in a strategic sense; because if you don't know where you are going in the long run it is very easy to go off course. As Tony Robbins a renowned motivational speaker put it "in ten years time you may not know what you want, but you will surely arrive!" It can seem like a waste of time to think ten years ahead but as Robbins has suggested while you are making up your mind about where you want to end up, you can wake up and realise ten years have passed.

Strategic goals can change but it is likely that your life purpose will always be with you. You may demonstrate or use it with different groups or in different situations, but the true essential you and your talents will be there. It is important to remember this when drawing up your long term vision about where your talents will take you. For instance a teacher who wants to share his/her subject with the world and be a successful business person may think that this is not how education works, education is supplied by the public sector; and simply accept that their aim must be to become a high level principal or administrative post. However the vision of Robert Kiyasaki, founder of the "rich dad/poor dad" brand which teaches financial literacy is interesting in this context. Robert is a teacher at heart but has created an online community which plays a game he uses to teach the principles of financial literacy. He also has a variety of information products which educate and conducts seminar tours, simply because he refused to limit his vision.

The Power of Goal Setting

You have no doubt read many times about the power of goal setting. Basically clearly defined goals tend to provide clearer direction and a greater chance of success. You need a list of goals for both short and long term, for most aspects of your life. For instance if your only goal was to have your own business by age 35, and to be earning £150,000 per year, the danger is that if this is your only focus, it may be the only thing you achieve and you could find yourself with no personal or social life as a consequence simply because you did not set goals for this area of your life. This may please the army of negative thinkers who use the 'lonely success' story as an example of why it is better not to have goals. However where goal setters, set targets in both their business and personal life, they can achieve success but not at any price, and still maintain a proper work life balance.

Do You Need to Pay a Price?

Depending on your goal there is a price to pay. I don't believe it has to be your social or family life. However you do have to remove a lot of things from your life that do conflict with your goals.

You need to avoid taking on too many outside projects which may conflict with your aim. However the power of goals lies in setting out clear targets against which you can measure your progress on the road to achieving your vision/life purpose.

Features and Goals

Goals should be positive, specific and measurable. For instance if you say "I would like to give up smoking in the near future" you are not following a couple of these conditions.

Firstly your goal is negative there is no specific timescale set to target the outcome. This is not a goal, but a vague aim which will be much more difficult to achieve.

What will I see, hear and feel to know that I have achieved my goal?

This implies a search for the sensory evidence that will tell you when you have achieved objectives.

What Will I Lose?

It is important to consider what benefits you are will actually gain from changing a specific aspect of your behaviour. When you are setting a goal it can be useful to question exactly why you want to achieve it. For instance you say you want a BMW Series Seven, a good question to ask yourself would be "why do I want it"? You may genuinely love German cars and really want this model, but if you find as you do on some occasions that you simply want to be respected and admired because you drive a BMW Series Seven, it is the feeling you want more than the actual car and it might be better to work on getting that feeling met.

Write Your Goals in Detail

Spell out the detail of each goal as this is important for visualisation, for your subconscious mind to accept it and to start finding opportunities to make it happen.

Level of Goals

You need goals that will 'stretch you' but are still achievable. If your main goal is to have lunch in a restaurant two days this month, this is very achievable and should not stretch you too much. However, if you want to become president of the USA by Friday that is most definitely pushing things too far. One of the key benefits of setting a goal and then working towards it, is the personal development this involves, i.e. what you will learn on your journey towards achieving it.

Key Goal

What one goal could have an impact on all aspects of your life? Which goal would be life changing? Goal setting should not be a one off exercise. It is something you do for the rest of your life. You should certainly have more than one.

Obstacles

There will be obstacles to the achieving of your goals. Some of these may come about because you may have a specific fear, while other obstacles will be provided by the outside world. What can be helpful is to anticipate and plan for them and even welcome them. Obstacles are part of the process of achievement and you have to deal with them on your way to achieving your targets. Ideally you want to find out as soon as possible what they are, and face them.

As we have noted already, not only do you want to achieve the goal, but you should ask yourself "what type of person do I have to become to achieve that goal"?

action and results

That is why people who achieve their goals despite the obstacles and have to stretch to achieve them, have an advantage over someone who achieves the same goal by luck. If you become a millionaire by business and financial strategies you will have developed a skill set which you can turn to again and again. Whereas if you become a millionaire by wining the lottery, ironically it may become another lottery determining whether you hold on to the money and prosper as the wealth is not a result of your own actions and skills development.

One Step at a Time

How do you eat an elephant? One bite at a time. Once you have set goals and I recommend 5 year/1 year, quarterly, weekly and daily goals, it is the actions you take that will achieve the results. Sometimes there will be an opportunity to make one significant breakthrough but usually it is a step by step process.

What Resources Do You Have?

It can be useful to identify what resources are needed to achieve your goals, and whether you have them now. Do you know the right people? Do you have money? What do you have going for you to help you attain your goals and what do you need to get?

> **TASK**
>
> Set out your goals for 5 years. Pick one in work, one in personal development and one in your personal life.

Do the same for yearly, quarterly, weekly and daily goals. Do your goals pass the test? Do you really want them? Keep a mini goals book and three times a day look at your goals list.

Review

Review both your goals and your performance on a regular basis. Do you still want the same things? Are you on target? What should you do differently in order to achieve your strategy?

Outcome/Thinking

You need to define your own personal goals and you should try where possible to ensure that these goals do not conflict with your business or work. You do need to consider the ecology of the situation. Is there any area of life which could be adversely affected if you achieve your goals? For instance if you have a young family and your goal is to travel and work abroad 28 days per month this is unlikely to leave a lot of time for your family and will cause pressures/conflicts. This is why it is important to discuss your goals with the people in your life. Their support or the lack of it will play a major part in your success.

Outcome/Orientation

In order to be effective you should always have an outcome orientation, i.e. you should have thought ahead about what result you want and acted accordingly. Let us say you get on the phone to speak to a prospective customer. It is important that you are clear about what you want from the call. You do not necessarily want or expect to make a sale over the phone. What you want is to make an appointment for a face to face presentation. Therefore you must ensure you do not try to sell your product/service too much over the phone and lose sight of your goal.

If you attend a networking event what do you want to achieve? If you go and stay with your best friend the whole evening you have failed Much better to have reviewed the guest list and set yourself a realistic target to meet four new people to include two people who could be customers for your company.

Thinking even for a moment about what you want to achieve tends to focus your mind on the key things and makes it less likely that you will waste time and lose focus. Meetings are famous for people getting drawn into discussions about irrelevant issues, and things going off on a tangent. Clearly, if there is a chairman it is their responsibility to keep to an agenda, however it is up to you as an individual to have your own outcome focus to ensure you get what you want to achieve from your attendance at the meeting.

action and results

The following well known issues are important:
    What positive outcome do you want?
    When specifically?
    How will you know you have achieved it?
    What resources do you need to gather?
    When will you review it?

There is a strong correlation between being 'results orientated' and taking action. Focusing on outcomes is a 20/80 activity that will increase the likelihood of you taking appropriate action.

You may get a little worried that you will be seen as one of those people who "always has an angle", or that people, particularly in your personal life may become resentful, or where every seemingly innocent conversation or action has a purpose or hidden agenda. You do need to switch off at times, but to maintain work/life balance the enterprising person needs to be making things happen, and therefore particularly in business does not want to waste any valuable opportunities which may be presented at conferences, business meetings or negotiations.

Action Overrated

I find it is really hard to know when the outcome setting ends and the action begins and vice versa. This is because outcome setting without action is a complete waste of time, but simply doing things for the sake of it is equally so. I am sure you have heard the quote that a definition of insanity is doing the same thing over and over again achieving the same result.

Focused action is the key but outcomes and action are part of that seamless loop we discussed earlier where outcomes are set, action taken, feedback monitored with action taken possibly modified to keep driving to meet the initial outcomes.

There is no doubt that what we are discussing is the second key feature of enterprising behaviour. We have talked about being creative curious and innovative to identify opportunities. Action is another feature in the equation. Sadly many people do not take action even when a golden opportunity is presented. Why? Let's discuss this.

Why Do People Not Take Action?

Firstly, without goals or outcomes it is difficult to take appropriate action. However there are a whole host of other reasons. Many of these have been already discussed in detail in this book.

Belief

> The importance of believing that you can change or influence people/situations.

Personal Mastery

> Lack of confidence and negative emotions such as fear of rejection or failure are often inhibiting factors.

Assertion

> Making sure you know the difference between aggression and assertiveness.

> By working on these "E Factor" skills you will increase your chances of taking effective action. It is easy at times to adopt negative habits such as procrastination, and that is why it is important, once you have defined a goal, you take a first small step towards achieving it.

Desire

> You may think you want the goal you have defined. Many people when asked to define a goal say they want to be a millionaire. If presented with a process or blueprint to achieve this goal most will say they would like the money, but not enough to be prepared to go outside their comfort zone to achieve it. Taking action and being proactive usually involves getting out of that zone.

TASK

What do you want to change in your life? Are you prepared to do something about it? Face Facts!

---

action and results

Inability to Think Strategically

Many of us are a bit like laboratory rats; provided we receive immediate reward or reinforcement for taking action we are keen to do so.
You must realise that there are some steps that will only make a difference in the long run; we don't necessarily receive a reward every
time we take action. There are often activities which are important
but not urgent but which will have a significant impact in the long
run.

"Paralysis Analysis"

Many highly educated people, academics and professionals will be
capable of analysing all the problems of a new project and of dissect-
ing a new opportunity. The problem is the more you do this, the more
you will identify challenges and uncertainties. However new proj-
ects/opportunities will always have uncertainties and part of the core
skill of the enterprising person is that once they have done their
homework and feel comfortable overall with the calculated risk they
will go for it!

Northern Ireland has one of the best Enterprise support networks in
the UK but also one of the lowest rates of start ups particularly
amongst women. We also have one of the best educational systems in
UK. 'INVEST NI' the local regional development agency has
allocated significant funding to a promotional campaign to urge the
population as a whole to "go for it". By providing road shows, role
models etc. they are hoping to change the culture by making people
aware of the availability of all the help they need.

However, much more focus is needed on improving action orientation for individuals. I feel that too much education and training for
entrepreneurs is awareness training and the provision of information.
My own view is that 'action learning' should play a bigger part and
that students and trainers should actually do things and practice the
behaviour skills outlined within this book. This is arguably much
more likely to lead to the start of a new project rather than information on the tax system and analysing a case study. Ironically many of
the people who lead the courses have never actually started a new
enterprise (successfully or not), and are therefore advising others to
go for something they haven't done themselves. They will try to

introduce role models who will help, but ultimately enterprise action needs to be taught or mentored by people who have very direct real life experiences to share.

The Inner and Outer Enemy

Your 'inner critic' will be one of your toughest opponents. You need to learn to override the fears that hold you back. Actually it is that first or second step, no matter how small that will help to lead to further action. Jealousy may even be a problem. When we see someone doing something we would not dare to do, instead of encouraging them and admiring them for their willingness to take action, there is almost a collective commitment to secretly hope that it doesn't work for them, if only to justify our own position.

So you can see there are lots of reasons why people avoid action. It is a lot easier to talk about doing something or even to show somebody else how to do it, than to do it ourselves.

So How Do We Turn You Into Action Man/Woman?

As you can see we can analyse why people avoid action ad infinitum. This is missing the point as people will often find a new excuse to show why they never get round to things.

As someone who is actively involved in encouraging people to come up with business ideas, people never seize to amaze me. I have proved time and again that creativity is an acquired skill, and I have been amazed by the quality of the ideas provided by the participants on my courses. It is not part of my remit to cajole them into turning the idea into reality but I think it may be time I moved into this area. So many of them having come up with the idea will barely consider even protecting their intellectual property rights in it. One group of participants last November devised a new piece of equipment for the hospitality business. I then noticed that the idea was identified as a great opportunity in The Sunday Times Business supplement. I went to see the group the next day and demanded that they get down to the patent office and explained how highly the idea was rated. "Maybe after our exams in February" was the reply. Needless to say it never happened. It does not make this group of participants, bad people. In fact they were very nice. For whatever reason they represent the silent majority who are clearly capable of coming up with great ideas/innovations but somehow never getting round to taking any action.

The Steps

So what should you do to become more action orientated?

The first thing I want you to do is every time you have a new idea. Do something no matter how small a step it is. If you want to start a new project buy a book about it – make a call!

Get a coach! A coach is not someone who advises you. Their role is to help you set up your own action plan and then do everything in their power to make you carry it out. They will ring, email, meet, inspire/push. Sometimes a paid coach is the answer. Your boss, bank manager boyfriend/girlfriend family may be too involved to be detached. You may be lucky to have a role model who does this for you as a friend. Getting a coach even for a short time will boost your capability of taking action.

Keep your word – From now on only agree to do something for somebody if you are 100% committed. If there is any uncertainty about your commitment then say no. What you are doing is training yourself to keep your word to yourself. This shows that you understand that when you say yes you will do something it is as good as done. This means a lot to customers, financiers etc and demonstrates your action orientation

'Chunk it down'! Break things into small manageable tasks and start doing it now

Persist! Take action but be relaxed about the outcome. Obstacles will appear. Stop, draw breath, take action again and find a way round the obstacle.

Reward – Build your 'why' up to increase self motivation. If you need to do something you don't want to, give yourself a small immediate reward for taking action.

Find what drives you – If you are doing this for your family, remind yourself at least once a day why you are taking action now.

Start today – Remember there is no tomorrow. Ask yourself every day, what action have I taken towards my goals?

Always keep your plan goals to hand. Look at them everyday at least once. You may only have five minutes free in the middle of all the fire fighting. Use it for something no matter how simple

Get any form of support or help you can

Work on your personal mastery – how do you see things? Do you see the project happening? Are you visualising it happening every day? Seek out a like minded person and support each other

Time Management: Make time to take some action everyday and keep a journal

Have weekly review sessions with yourself to monitor the process Learn self discipline! Practice self discipline! Even if you want to start on a diet, or begin daily exercise, things that you have been putting off. For instance let's take exercise. Start off with 5 minutes simple exercise every day. Doesn't seem much but every day you must make time for it. Build up gradually to fifteen minutes every day. Not only will this help your health and energy but again you are playing games with the subconscious mind. You are showing that you have self discipline and can make yourself do something every day. It doesn't matter what your focus is, you are practising self discipline. Some of you may have this quality already. For the rest of us it is the unpleasant part of turning any idea into a reality. Constantly attack your comfort zones. If you are doing something which is an easy routine, find something different to do.

TASK

List three comfort zones you have. Attack one of them

Adopt a motto/affirmation – Use something like "just do it" get yourself a paradigm that works for you "I will take action" "I will make it happen", "action is the key". I was inspired to write this book and have done so in less than a month after reading Jeffrey Archer's Prison Journals. "Strange" you may say, but despite the harsh prison regime Jeffrey Archer made himself get up at 5 o'clock every morning to write for two hours. Of all the traits self discipline is the one you must master. It is related to motivation but where self discipline kicks in is when the motivation to do something is not yet there but you still do what you have to do anyhow.

Find Motivational Aids – there may be a movie or a sporting event which motivates you, a piece of music. I am rather partial to anything that reminds me of" Rocky". If you have got to take action, maybe do something which includes a confrontation you would rather avoid. Try remembering a role model who was able to confront a big problem. What would they do? How would they act?

Act Confidently: You may feel less than confident. However moving confidently and acting confidently will not only give the outside world the appearance of confidence, but will also help you to take action.

Find your own motivation strategy. It may be you only really get moving when you are facing imminent disaster. You need to then visualise all the dire consequences you will face if you do not take action. Sometimes people wait until external circumstances push too far before they will take action. Create the circumstances yourself.

Keep an action journal – At the start of every day – ask yourself "What three things will I do today to move my life forward?" At the end of everyday record faithfully whether you did anything or not

Only get interested in profound knowledge, i.e. knowledge that you can apply to your everyday life. If you are studying Business strategy or attending a seminar on innovation, ask yourself what one idea from this lecture can I go and use now?

People always say that information is power. However information is only of any use if action is taken. If you sincerely want to develop your enterprise capability you are in fact on a mission to improve your ability to take action, otherwise known as personal power. Knowledge of a skill is of little use because it is not part of your normal behaviour. The only way to inspire is to start practising every day. Having a do it now attitude is good. You need to work on your E Factors Daily – Practice the skills until they are part of you without thinking. To me there is nothing more cruel than possessing knowledge or opportunity but letting the opportunity slip by.

Work on your state. Try to get into the action frame of mind. Usually you will feel empowered, in the right state, with belief you can do it now

Model the people who take action. What is it about their beliefs, their thoughts and physiology that you could copy? Look at world leaders but also look at successful local entrepreneurs or community leaders.

Be Congruent. Make sure your voice, tonality, posture all match up You need energy. At times you will have limited opportunity to take the action you need. If you are tired or run down you will find it physically difficult to do what you know you should. Sensible diet, sleep and exercise patterns will help together with working at relaxation so that stress will drain less of your energy away.

Listen to William Shakespeare in The Merchant of Venice "If to do were as easy as to know what were good to do chapels would be churches and poor men's cottages princes palaces" Where you are now in life is a direct result of all the action you have taken to date. The chances are that if you repeat the same action you will end up getting the same results. You need to realise that you may not always feel positive but continue to take positive action. Performing an act of random kindness can help. If someone is struggling with a trolley help them

Limit your actions to the key 20% that make the difference. Don't waste your action muscles on unnecessary activity. Only take action where you can have an impact.

Take action on one area of your life at a time – that area that is bothering you most. Find the key breakthrough things you must do and concentrate on them. Draw up a schedule showing aims, action sequences and action start dates.

action and results

Don't waste time! Get into action. Every day you contemplate is a day wasted. Research and analysis is useful but you will learn from action that things happen, some good some bad. If you can be flexible in your responses you can then take appropriate action. The momentum you create will open up opportunities for you. Time is your greatest resource, every day you do not take focused action is a day wasted. The most successful entrepreneurs I have met were not necessarily workaholics. They used their time well. During 9-5 they took action. They took the actions where they made the most impact. They then enjoyed their private lives after that.

What three actions could you take now that could have the most leverage in your life? Do them today not tomorrow. As is often said, anyone can do it. They can if they set their outcomes that they want from life at a macro and micro level and take focused action, respond where the desired result is not being immediately achieved and adapt in order to achieve results. A great Enterprise person will have the personal power to take action when it is necessary. Like a tiger on the prowl they will seem relaxed, watching what is happening however when the timing is right they will put all their energy into positive focused attention.

Do it now! Don't delay. Always plan ahead! Look for what you want then act on it. Roll with the punches and keep taking action until your goals are achieved. Go for it!

Conclusion

So we have reached the end or is it the beginning?

I hope you realise that you can be more enterprising and improve your "E Factor" wherever you are now.

There are a few key things you must do to take the ideas you have looked at here and apply them to your life.

Visit out website www.efactor.eu and do our E Factor assessment tests.

Decide which of the E Competencies you need to work on

Do something today!
Pick 2 ideas to work on
Constantly search for opportunities. Keep a
journal and learn
Email us once a month

Remember I am your E Coach

If you could just take one idea from each chapter and make it part of your life, you could make a massive change. Let us help, work on your key efactors and see the change in your world. You were born to be Enterprising. It is time to do something about it. Do it now!

action and results

BIBLIOGRAPHY

Buzan, Tony (2001) **The Power of Creative Intelligence**: Harper Collins

Covey, Stephen (1999) **Seven Habits of Highly Effective People**. Simon & Schuster: New York

De Bono, Edward., (1990) **The Use of Lateral Thinking**: Penguin Books.

Kennedy, Gavin(1997) **Everything is Negotiable**: Random House Business Books.

Kiyosaki, Robert; Lechter, Sharon L. (1997) **Rich Dad Poor Dad**: Warner Books.

La Salle, Roger (2002) Think New. Rudders RLS Pty. Ltd. Victoria, Australia.

Ryan, Dave Marshall, (1999) **The Streetwise Guide to Starting your Own Business**: Streetwise Publications.

Senge, Peter M. (1990) **The Fifth Discipline; the Art and Practice of the Learning Organization**. Doubleday: USA.

Silverman, George (2000) **The Secrets of Word of Mouth Marketing**: AMACON.

Sugar, Sir Alan (2005) **The Apprentice**: BBC Books.

Thompson, Geoff (2001) **The Great Escape - The 10 Secrets to Loving your Life and Living your Dreams**: Summersdale.

Trump, Donald. (1989) **The Art of the Deal**: Warner Books: New York.

Wilde, Stuart (1995) **The Trick to Money is Having None**: Hay House.